The OXFORD Children's A to Z of Music

Humphrey Carpenter • Paul Keene • Christine Wood

OXFORD UNIVERSITY PRESS

OXFORD
UNIVERSITY PRESS

Great Clarendon Street, Oxford OX2 6DP

Oxford University Press is a department of the University of Oxford. It furthers the University's objective of excellence in research, scholarship, and education by publishing worldwide in

Oxford New York

Auckland Cape Town Dar es Salaam Hong Kong Karachi Kuala Lumpur Madrid Melbourne Mexico City Nairobi New Delhi Shanghai Taipei Toronto

With offices in

Argentina Austria Brazil Chile Czech Republic France Greece Guatemala Hungary Italy Japan Poland Portugal Singapore South Korea Switzerland Thailand Turkey Ukraine Vietnam

Oxford is a registered trade mark of Oxford University Press in the UK and in certain other countries

First published 1997

This edition 2004

British Library Cataloguing in Publication Data

Data available

ISBN-13: 978-0-19-911255-5
ISBN-10: 0-19-911255-X

10 9 8 7 6 5 4 3 2
Printed in Thailand

Acknowledgements

Design and art editing: Vivienne Gordon
Picture research: Image Select International (London)
Photographs
The publishers would like to thank the following for permission to reproduce photographs:
AKG (London): 7tr, 12b, 22tl, 24tr, 26tr, 33bl; **Aquarius:** 6/7; **Art Directors:** 61; **Boosey and Hawkes (London):** 24bcr, 24br, 25ltc, 25bl; **Bridgeman Art Library:** 16/17, 61; **J Allan Cash:** 56; **City of Birmingham Symphony Orchestra:** 39t; **Decca Music:** 10b; **Zoe Dominic/Catherine Ashmore:** 45t, 58b; **Mary Evans:** 29t, 33bl; **Ronald Grant:** 33t; **Hoa-Qui:** 62b; **Hutchison Picture Library:** 19; **Images Colour Library:** 63br; **Images of India:** 15t; **Image Select:** 4, 7br, 8bl, 10, 12t, 20t, 25tr, 25ltc, 27cl, 28b, 51t; **Image Select/Sampers:** 49; **Image Select/Kennercy:** 58t; **Kobal Collection:** 8/9, 15t, 46; **Lebrecht Collection:** 53; **London Features International:** 22br, 42t, 43, 45b, 48, 51b; **Magenta Music International:** 40/41; **Performing Arts Library:** 9tr, 29b, 46/47, 59; **C F Peters Corporation, New York; Peters Edition Ltd, London:** 20b; **Redferns:** 4/5, 14tl, 17br, 18bl, 23, 25t, 26tc, 26bc, 26br, 28t, 30t, 32, 42b, 47b, 50; **Rex Features:** 11l, 13b, 14/15, 21b, 32, 36, 54, 60; **Keith Saunders:** 38/39; **Science Photo Library:** 11r; **South American Pictures:** 64l; **Spectrum Colour Library:** 18tr, 24bl, 63bl; **Thomas Photo:** 25br; **Reg Wilson:** 57; **Yamaha Music:** 17t, 21r, 24tc, 24rc, 24bc, 25lbc

Illustrations
James Alexander: 5, 6tr, 9b, 23r, 33br, 44; **Michael Courtney:** 55tr; **Clive Goodyer:** 6tl, 10t, b; **Edward McLachlan:** 16tl; **Andy Parker:** 15cl, 50, 53; **Helen Parsley:** 14t, 21tr, 26cl, 31cb, 40br, 48, 60cr, 61cl, 62cr, 63cr, 64tr; **Martin Sanders:** 63t, 64t; **Keith Smith:** 7br, 18br, 19bl, 37, 62cl

Every effort has been made to trace copyright holders. Where this has not been possible, the publishers apologise and would like to hear from any copyright holder not acknowledged.

Dear Reader

At this very moment, someone somewhere – perhaps on the other side of the world – may be listening to your favourite piece of music. Perhaps it's rave music, a sonata by Mozart, or a folk tune played on a zither. The sound may be coming from a CD player, a radio, or someone may be performing it live.

Music is one of the greatest pleasures in life. It can make you feel happy or sad; it can make you want to dance or send you off to sleep. And everyone can do something musical, whether it be a child clapping in time to a nursery rhyme, a football fan singing at a match, or a pianist filling a huge concert hall with glorious tunes.

This book is for you to read about the different instruments people play, about how music is written down, and about the people who compose and perform it. Most important of all, this book will help you to enjoy listening to music. Wherever you see the CD sign it means there is a suggestion for something interesting to listen to.

Why not start right now by looking through the book and reading whatever catches your eye, or try listening to a piece you've never heard before? It could be the start of a whole new musical life for you!

Slow, grand music sounds magnificent in the echoing acoustic of a huge cathedral.

accompaniment

An accompaniment is the music which supports the main singer or player.

In pop music the accompaniment is usually called the backing.

acoustic

A concert hall or church has a good acoustic if you can hear the sound clearly. Too much echo muddles musical sounds up with each other. Without any echo at all, music sounds thin, dry and boring. The study of how sound behaves is called 'acoustics'.

An acoustic instrument (for example an acoustic guitar) is one that produces its sounds naturally, not electronically.

alto

Alto is the name of a voice or an instrument with a medium to high range. Alto is pitched below soprano and above tenor.
See also **counter-tenor**, **voice**.

anthem

An anthem is a short piece of religious music. It is usually performed by the choir and organ at church services. There are all sorts of anthems for special occasions like weddings, funerals and coronations. Each country in the world also has its own 'national anthem'. This is usually a solemn song with patriotic words.

One of the most famous anthems is *Zadok the Priest*, by Handel. He wrote it in 1727 for the coronation of King George II of England.

aria

An aria is a song for a single singer accompanied by an orchestra. In operas or oratorios the main characters sing arias to explain their thoughts and feelings. Arias are often the best-known bits of operas.
See also **recitative**.

The aria 'Nessun Dorma' (which means 'No one sleeps') became a hit in 1990, when it was used as the TV theme tune for the football World Cup. It was sung by Luciano Pavarotti, and comes from Puccini's opera *Turandot*.

Armstrong, Louis

(1901–1971)

Louis Armstrong was one of the greatest jazz musicians. He was born into a poor family in New Orleans, USA. After he fired a gun in the street as a joke, he was sent to a children's home. There he learned to play the trumpet.

When he left the home he played in bands on boats going up and down the Mississippi River. Then he formed his own group, the Louis Armstrong Hot Five. He was also a singer and songs like 'Hello Dolly' made his gravelly voice world-famous.
See also **blues**, **jazz**.

Louis Armstrong's amazing trumpet solos inspired many other jazz musicians.

arpeggio

When the notes of a **chord** are played one after the other (instead of together), they are called an arpeggio. Arpeggios can go upwards or downwards.

Like scales, arpeggios are one of the basic building-blocks of music.

arranger

An arranger is someone who rewrites music that was originally composed for another instrument, or for voice. Many popular jazz pieces are arrangements of songs for instruments. You will be able to find a song like 'Yesterday', by the Beatles, arranged for choir, piano, orchestra, recorders and even steel band.

audition

An audition is a kind of test. If you want to be in a choir, orchestra or band you often have to sing or play in front of other people. Then they can decide if you are good enough to join. Sometimes an audition can be more scary than a real performance!

Bach, Johann Sebastian

(1685–1750)

J.S. Bach was the greatest composer of **baroque** music, and a famous German organist. At first he was taught music by his father. When he was nine his parents died and his elder brother took over. Bach began his career as a choirboy, later working as a musician for the Duke of Weimar and Prince Leopold of Cöthen. For the last 27 years of his life he was a busy choirmaster, teacher and church organist, writing impressive church music like the *St Matthew Passion*.

Bach had 20 children, and wrote some of his smaller pieces to help them practise their instruments. Two of his sons, Carl Phillipp Emmanuel and Johann Christian, later became famous composers themselves.

There is a story that a French organist challenged Bach to a musical duel on the organ. When he heard Bach practising on the night before the competition, he was so terrified that he packed his bags and fled.

Some of Bach's most exciting music can be found in the six *Brandenburg Concertos*. No. 2 has a thrilling high trumpet part, and the first movement of No. 5 gives the harpsichordist a tremendous opportunity to show off.

ballet

See **dance music**.

barbershop quartet

A barbershop quartet is a group of four male singers. Barbershop songs are often sweet, slow and romantic. Nowadays there are also female barbershop quartets called 'Sweet Adelines'.

Barbershop got its name because in Shakespeare's time men waiting for a haircut used to pass the time singing.

Barbershop singers wear snazzy clothes. They learn their music by heart so that they can burst into song at any moment.

baritone

Baritone is the name of a male voice (or instrument) that is fairly low. Baritone is below **tenor** and above **bass**.
See also **voice**.

baroque music

European music written between about 1600 and 1750 is often called baroque music. The word means 'richly decorated' and was originally used to describe the architecture of the time. The most famous composers of baroque music are Bach, Handel and Vivaldi.

Bartók, Béla

(1881–1945)

One music critic said that listening to Bartók's music was worse than going to the dentist!

Bartók was a Hungarian composer. He used folk music to help him develop his own style. At first people found his music harsh and modern because of its **discords**, and it was rarely performed. In 1940, at the start of the Second World War, Bartók emigrated to the USA. He died there a few years later, ill and homesick, just before his music became widely popular.

Bartok's *Romanian Folk Dances* show how he captured the spirit of folk music with colourful use of instruments and lively dance rhythms.

bass

Bass is the lowest male voice. The word is also used to describe a low instrument, like the bass clarinet. The bass line is the lowest part in any music.
See also **voice**.

beat

Most music is kept going by a regular pulse which is called the beat. It keeps going steadily under the music, like your heartbeat or the ticking of a clock.

In some music you can feel the beat strongly. **Rock music** has a very heavy beat. Dance music often has a strong, fast beat, while a march usually has a slow beat, to match the pace of walking.

Beatles

The Beatles were probably the most important group in the history of pop music. Their catchy tunes and lively personalities caught the excitement of the 1960s, and Beatlemania created a boom in British pop. The group's members were John Lennon, Paul McCartney, George Harrison and Ringo Starr. John and Paul wrote most of the songs, some of which were about their home town, Liverpool.

The group split up in 1970, and John Lennon was shot dead in New York in 1980.

In 1995 a new Beatles track was released called 'Free as a Bird'. It used a tape recording of a song which John Lennon had made before he died, adding the other voices and instruments to it.

Try 'Yesterday', and 'Yellow Submarine'.

The Beatles were nicknamed the 'Fab Four' because of their amazing success.

Beethoven, Ludwig van

(1770–1827)

Beethoven was a composer and a brilliant pianist, but he began to go deaf in his mid-twenties. This ended his piano-playing career, and as his deafness grew worse he became difficult and bad-tempered. But he overcame his despair with braveness and determination.

When Beethoven became deaf people had to write down their conversations for him. He continued to compose by hearing the music in his head.

Beethoven's music is often heroic and noble, and it reflects his struggles in life. His music was more powerful than anything composed before, and he was a great influence on later composers.

The opening bars of Beethoven's Fifth Symphony are some of the best-known in all music, and have been called 'Fate knocking at the door'.

bell

Bells are hollow metal objects that chime when they are struck. Some bells are hit from the outside with a hammer. Others are struck from inside by a piece of metal called a 'clapper'. For thousands of years, bells have been used in religious ceremonies all over the world. Very large bells are often given names. 'Great Tom' is the bell which peals the time in Big Ben, the famous clock outside the Houses of Parliament in London.

Berlin, Irving

(1888–1989)

Irving Berlin was one of the best songwriters of the 20th century. He was born in Russia, but his family went to live in the USA when he was five. They were very poor, and Irving worked as a street busker and as a singing waiter when still a boy. By his late teens his songs were being published and he swept to fame during the **ragtime** craze in the early 1900s. Berlin lived to the age of 101 and published over 1,500 songs. For much of his life he could not read music, and other people had to write it down for him.

Bernstein's *West Side Story* is a version of Shakespeare's love story *Romeo and Juliet*. It is brought up to date and set in the gang warfare of 20th-century New York.

Berlioz, Hector

(1803–1869)

The French composer Hector Berlioz was the son of a doctor. Although his father wanted him to study medicine, Hector could not stand the sight of blood and wanted to be a musician. People thought his music was peculiar because it was so original. He believed that music should express the composer's feelings as powerfully as possible.

The *Symphonie Fantastique* (meaning 'Fantastical Symphony') contains a wildly exciting movement called the Witches' Sabbath, as well as a nightmarish March to the Scaffold.

People made fun of Berlioz's music because it often required gigantic choirs and orchestras.

Bernstein, Leonard

(1918–1890)

Leonard Bernstein was an American conductor and composer. His best-known composition is the thrilling musical *West Side Story*. Bernstein's vivid music mixes together all sorts of interesting styles like jazz, musicals, and Latin-American dance rhythms.

big band

A big band is a large jazz group of trumpets, trombones, saxophones, piano, guitar and double bass. Big bands (also called 'swing bands') became popular in the 1930s, playing the dance hits of the day.

A good starting point for big band music is the Duke **Ellington** Band's 'Take the A Train'.

Bizet, Georges

(1838–1875)

Bizet was a French composer. He is best known for *Carmen*, one of the world's most popular operas. It is the tragic story of the gypsy girl Carmen and her rival lovers, a soldier and a toreador (Spanish bullfighter). Oddly enough, the opera was not an instant success. Bizet died soon after the first performances, unaware that he had written one of the greatest opera hits of all time.

Try listening to 'Habanera' and 'Toreador's Song' from *Carmen*.

Bizet's opera Carmen *is dramatic and exciting, overflowing with wonderful tunes and colourful Spanish atmosphere.*

blues

Blues is a melancholy style of **jazz**. Its slow, plodding tunes and sliding harmonies express feeling 'blue', which means unhappy. Blues developed from the folk music of black Africans, who had been sold into slavery in America. It has influenced many other styles of jazz and pop. A 12-bar blues is a simple pattern of **chord**s which players use to improvise around.
See also Billie **Holiday**, **improvisation**.

Listen to the 'St Louis Blues' (Bessie Smith singing, with Louis **Armstrong** on trumpet).

boogie-woogie

Boogie-woogie is a style of jazz piano-playing. The pianist's left hand repeats a swinging rhythm. It's hard to describe in words, but you'll know it when you hear it!

Boogie-woogie developed in noisy American beer bars, where the pianos were so worn out that notes had to be played several times before they could be heard properly!

Brahms, Johannes

(1833–1897)

Brahms was a German composer. He came from a poor family, and in his teens earned money playing the piano in bars and dance halls. He became famous when the composer Robert **Schumann** wrote an article calling him a genius. Brahms much admired the symphonies of **Beethoven**, and it took him a long time to find enough confidence to write four marvellous symphonies of his own. He was a shy, modest man, whose gruffness masked passionate feelings that overflow in his warm-hearted, tuneful music.

Brahms was a great friend of Robert Schumann and his wife Clara. When Robert went mad, Brahms helped Clara through the crisis. He was secretly in love with her, though he never declared his feelings.

Listen to the last movement of Brahms' First Symphony, with its magnificent horn-call and stately march tune.

brass band

A brass band is a large group of brass instruments. Countries like England, Germany and Switzerland have a particularly strong tradition of brass bands. Brass bands are sometimes linked to schools or church groups like the Salvation Army, and the players often wear special uniforms.

Try the impressive first movement of Elgar's *Severn Suite.*

English brass bands were set up in the 19th century as a popular hobby for workers in factories and coal mines.

brass instruments

See **instruments** (brass family).

Britten, Benjamin

(1913–1976)

Britten was an English composer, and his talents were obvious at an early age. He spent most of his life by the sea. It was a great influence on his music, particularly the opera that made him world-famous, *Peter Grimes*. This is the tragic story of a fisherman who is cruel to the boys who work for him.

Britten thought that composers should be useful in society, and loved writing music for children and ordinary people. In 1958 he wrote *Noye's Fludde*. It is the musical story of Noah's ark, with parts for children to sing, play and act together with adults.

Britten's *Young Person's Guide to the Orchestra* is a wonderful musical demonstration of all the instruments of the orchestra. It was specially written for children.

Many of Britten's songs and operas were inspired by the voice of his lifelong partner, the singer Peter Pears (right).

busking

Busking is earning money by playing music in the street or in other public places. In jazz, busking means playing something by ear or by guesswork, rather than from written music.

C

cadenza

A cadenza is a short and elaborate bit of music in a **concerto**. It is written specially for the soloist to show off without the orchestra.
A cadenza comes near the end of a **movement**, and usually ends with a **trill** that warns the orchestra to get ready to play again.

calypso

A calypso is a type of West Indian folk song, often played by **steel bands**. Calypsos have catchy tunes and a special lilting rhythm. Calypsos developed when slaves were forbidden to talk as they worked in the plantation fields. They would sing the latest news to each other instead.

The world's most famous carol service takes place every Christmas Eve at King's College Chapel, Cambridge, in England. It is heard on the radio by millions of people.

carol

A carol is a simple religious song, usually with a number of verses and a chorus. Traditionally, carols were sung to celebrate European festivals like Christmas, New Year, Spring and Easter. Nowadays, though, a carol is usually just a Christmas song.

If you go carol-singing at Christmas, you probably use a mixture of ancient and modern carols from over 500 years. 'The holly and the ivy', for example, is probably very old, whilst 'Once in royal David's city' dates from Victorian times. There are all sorts of colourful modern carols, including 'The donkey carol' and the 'Calypso carol'.

CD

A CD (Compact Disc) is a round, flat piece of aluminium coated with plastic. When music is recorded onto a CD, sounds are converted into a code. When you play a CD, a laser beam inside the CD player scans the disc and converts the information back into sound.
See also **recording**, **sound**.

A CD stores coded information about sound in the form of millions of tiny pits in its aluminium surface.

chamber music

Music that can be played in a small room (a 'chamber') is sometimes called chamber music. Chamber music is played by groups of two to ten players and usually has just one player to a part. Classical composers like Haydn wrote a lot of chamber music, particularly string quartets, to play with their friends.
See also **trio**, **quartet**, **quintet**.

choir

A choir is a group of people who sing together. The singers sing different musical parts depending on how high or low their voices are. You don't always have to be able to read music to sing in a choir, as singers sometimes learn their parts by ear. But you will have to attend regular **rehearsals** to practise.

Music for choirs ranges from hymns and grand religious music to little rounds, folk songs and versions of pop songs. It is called choral music.
See also **chorus, oratorio, religious music**.

chord

A chord is any group of two or more notes played at the same time. The number of notes between any two notes in a chord is called an interval. Lots of standard chords have names, such as D7 and E minor. Guitarists and jazz musicians often play by **busking** from the chord names.
See also **discord, harmony**.

chorus

The chorus is the part of a **song** that is repeated after each verse and has the same words all the way through. It is sometimes called the refrain. If the verse is sung by one person, often everyone joins in for the chorus. A large choir is also sometimes called a chorus, as is the choir in operas and musicals.

The Mormon Tabernacle Choir, one of the world's biggest choirs, pictured in front of their enormous organ.

Chopin, Frédéric

(1810–1849)

Chopin was a Polish composer and pianist. He lived in Paris, teaching and composing piano music for his own performances. He never forgot his homeland, though, and used Polish dances in many of his shorter pieces. Chopin's piano music is some of the finest ever written. It often has unforgettably beautiful tunes that sing out over a rich accompaniment.

Listen to the angry and powerful 'Revolutionary' Study, and the dreamily sad Nocturne in B flat minor.

Much of Chopin's music was written for himself to play at concerts in the homes of rich aristocrats.

classical music

Classical music is the name generally used for the most formal kinds of music. Western classical music includes anything that is not pop, jazz or light music. It is usually carefully composed and written down, with less improvisation than pop or jazz. India and Asia have their own classical music too. It is often performed in religious settings according to traditional rules.

Classical music is also used specifically to mean European music written between 1750 and 1830. The most famous composers of this sort of classical music are **Haydn**, **Mozart** and **Beethoven**.

composer

A composer is a person who invents music. Sometimes composers make up their music at a keyboard, and sometimes they compose in their heads before writing it down.

Western classical composers write down exactly what they want to be played. In jazz, pop and non-western music, the composer is often the performer. So they may just write down a rough sketch and then improvise from it. It helps if composers know about music **theory** and also understand all the various musical instruments and how they sound best.
See also **improvisation**, **harmony**, **score**.

concert

A concert is an event where an audience comes specially to listen to live music. Concerts can be large or small. Concerts of Indian classical music often consist of improvisations lasting for many hours, creating a magical, hypnotic atmosphere.

Pop concerts are often held in huge stadiums with spectacular special effects accompanying the music. Jazz and folk groups perform in clubs or pubs, while classical concerts tend to be more formal. A classical concert given by a solo performer is called a 'recital'.

concerto

A concerto is a piece of music in which a single instrument (played by the soloist) is accompanied by an orchestra. Concertos usually show off the skill of a **virtuoso** performer, and they are often very difficult to play. The soloist's part displays the full range of sounds and moods of the instrument, and is contrasted with the orchestra's part in a dramatic and exciting way.

Most concertos have three **movements**. The first and last are fast, and the middle one is slow.
See also **cadenza**.

 Try Mozart's Horn Concerto No. 4, or Rodrigo's *Concierto de Aranjuez* (Guitar Concerto).

▽

In 1985 a massive charity concert was held at Wembley Stadium in London. It was called Live Aid and all the pop and rock groups performed free for charity. It was organized by Bob Geldof.

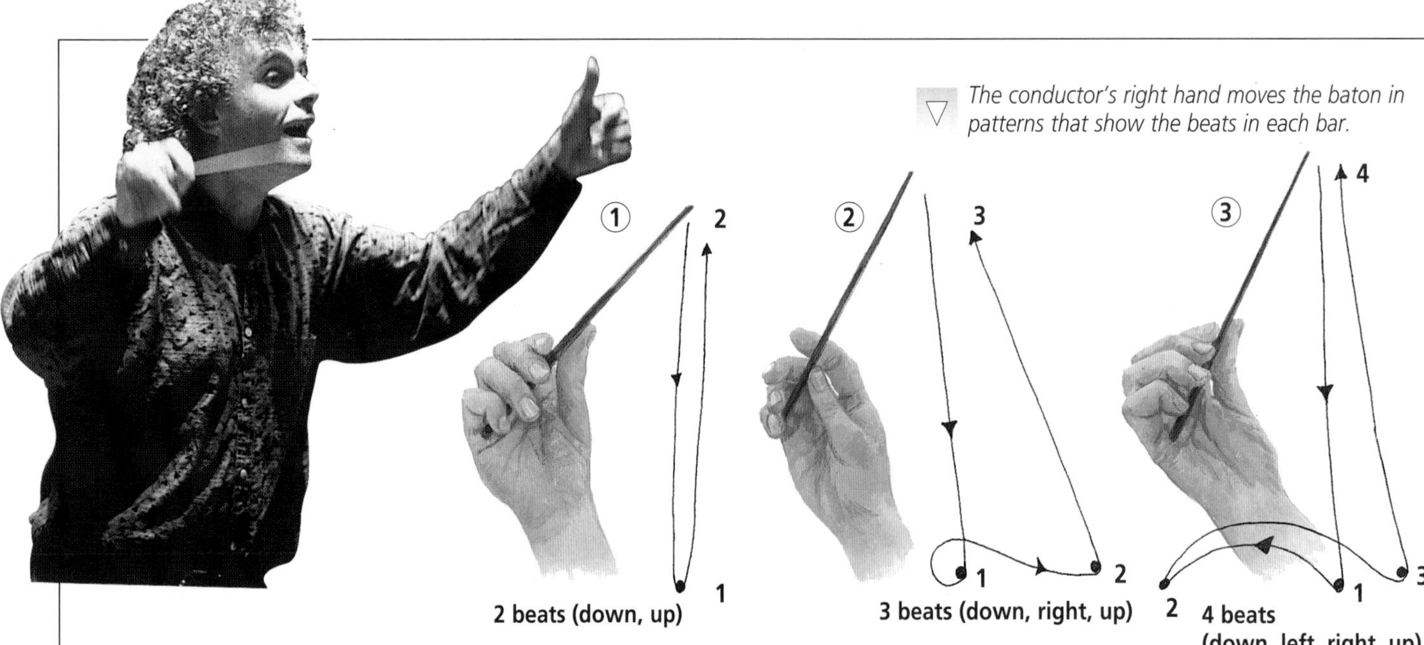

▽ *The conductor's right hand moves the baton in patterns that show the beats in each bar.*

△ *The conductor can't speak when the music is playing, so he or she will use facial expressions as well as hand movements to communicate with the players. The conductor here is Simon Rattle.*

conductor

A conductor is the person you will see beating time in front of a choir or orchestra. The conductor helps everyone keep in time together and makes sure that the different instruments play at the correct volume. He or she needs to know how each instrument works. During **rehearsals**, a conductor practises with the players, explaining how the piece should be performed.

A conductor usually stands on a raised platform called a rostrum, to be easily seen by the whole orchestra. A conductor's right hand beats time with a short white stick called a baton. The left hand is used to interpret the music – to set the mood, to show how loud or softly it should be played, and to help the players play expressively.

Every conductor has different ideas about how the music should sound. Some are more restrained, while others (like the great Leonard **Bernstein**) prefer the extremes of emotion. Modern conductors are often famous celebrities, flying round the world to conduct the top orchestras.

Conducting can be a risky business. A French composer called Lully hit his own foot when beating time by thumping a stick on the floor. It became infected, causing his death a few weeks later.

Copland, Aaron

(1900–1990)

Copland was an American composer. His early music was sometimes modern and difficult to listen to. In the 1930s he started writing more tuneful pieces. He created a style that sounded really American by using US folk songs, hymn tunes and jazz.

Copland's ballets *Billy the Kid* and *Rodeo* have vivid cowboy music to match their colourful stories.

counter-tenor

A counter-tenor is a man who sings at an **alto** pitch. Counter-tenors produce their high voices by tightening their vocal chords and singing 'falsetto'.
See also **voice**.

country and western

Country and western, or country music, is the most popular music in the southern USA. It started around the time of the American gold rush in the mid-19th century as a mixture of cowboy songs and folk songs. 'Hill billy' and 'bluegrass music' are kinds of country music. They are played on folk-music instruments like fiddles and banjos.

D

dance music

All over the world people love to dance, and there are many different kinds of dance music. All dance music has a strong rhythm or **beat** that makes our bodies want to move in time to it. The way we dance has to fit in with the music, whether it is elegant ballroom dancing, leaping Scottish dancing, or the tiny, graceful hand movements of Indian classical dance.

The most formal type of western dance is called ballet. It takes place on a stage and the music is played by an orchestra. Ballet usually tells a story in dance and music. The person who creates the dancing to go with the music is called the choreographer.
See also **flamenco**, **minuet**, **waltz**.

The best-known composer of ballet music is **Tchaikovsky**. Try his music for the ballets *Swan Lake* and *The Nutcracker*.

▽ *A modern production of Tchaikovsky's ballet* Swan Lake.

Debussy, Claude

(1862–1918)

Debussy was a French composer. He revolutionized classical music with his soft floating harmonies and delicate use of instruments. Many of his pieces have mysterious poetic titles and paint pictures in sound. His music is sometimes called 'impressionist' because it gives a dreamy impression of its subject.

Listen to the musical impression of a submerged cathedral in the piano piece *La Cathédrale Engloutie* ('The Drowned Cathedral') – can you hear the bells tolling and the choir chanting from beneath the waves?

descant

A descant is a special high part, usually for voices, which is sometimes added to the last verses of hymns and carols.
See also **recorder**.

discord

A discord is a combination of two or more notes that sound unpleasant together. Exactly what 'unpleasant' means is a matter of opinion. For example, some people find modern classical music discordant, while others enjoy it very much. Composers use discords to express pain and sadness, and to create tension.
See also **chord**.

drone

A drone is a low note that is held continuously throughout a piece of music. Listen to the bagpipes and you'll hear that they can produce a long, low drone note while also playing livelier tunes above it.

duet

A duet (or duo) is a piece of music played or sung by two performers.

There is a famous comic duet in which two women sing like cats howling in the night.

early music

Early music is a term used to describe western music that was composed before about 1750, from the music of medieval times up to **baroque music**. Early music is often played on instruments typical of the time when it was composed. These make the music sound lighter than modern instruments do, and let it dance along with more bounce. Early music groups put on early operas using historical scenery and costumes – sometimes even by candlelight!

Paintings can often tell us about the sorts of instruments used in the past. This one shows Italian musicians of the 16th century. The instrument played like a guitar is a lute, and the woman standing up is playing a recorder. The instrument that looks like a modern cello is called a viol, and the keyboard instrument that looks like a harpsichord is called a virginal.

Dvorák, Antonín

(1841–1904)

Dvorák was a Czech composer who was the son of a village butcher. But he neglected his father's trade to have music lessons, later earning his living as a viola player. Dvorák was very influenced by his country's folk music, which gives his own music lilting tunes and lively, dance-like rhythms. When he became famous he travelled a lot to Britain and America, but remained a modest man of simple tastes.

Dvorák's best-known piece, the *New World* Symphony, was written when he was in New York. It was intended to be a portrait of the United States, but you can tell the composer was deeply homesick from the emotional slow movement.

dynamics

The dynamics of music are how loudly or quietly it is played. If you use a variety of dynamics your playing will be more expressive. In written music dynamics are shown by words, letters and symbols.
See **notation**.

electronic music and instruments

Musical sounds can be produced electronically as well as by traditional instruments. Some composers invent completely new electronic sounds. Others record existing sounds like birdsong and then electronically transform them in all sorts of unusual ways. Most concerts of electronic music involve a combination of computers, tape machines and live performers.

Electronic instruments like the synthesizer are computers that store information about sound. They reproduce it electronically, by converting electrical energy into sound.

Instruments like the electric guitar and electric violin produce their sounds naturally, but amplify them (make them louder) electronically.
See also **recording**.

Nearly all pop recordings now use electronic drum or rhythm machines instead of real drum kits. When you listen it is hard to tell the difference.

Elgar, Edward

(1857–1934)

The English composer Edward Elgar came from an ordinary background. He worked in his father's music shop, teaching himself about music, and for a long time he was an unknown violin teacher. His *Enigma Variations* made him famous at the age of 42. Each of the **variations** is a musical picture of one of his friends, and the last one portrays the composer himself. Success gave Elgar confidence, and he became England's best-loved composer.

Elgar is popular for noble melodies like the *Pomp and Circumstance March No. 1* ('Land of Hope and Glory'), and a sweet sadness that is best heard in his Cello Concerto.

Ellington, Duke

(1899–1974)

Edward Ellington was a famous jazz band leader, pianist and composer. As a young man, his smart, stylish dress sense earned him the nickname 'Duke'. Starting in the 1930s **swing** era, he led the Duke Ellington big band for 45 years.

Duke Ellington's hit tunes like 'Don't Get around Much Anymore' and 'Mood Indigo' have never gone out of fashion.

Duke Ellington seated at the piano, smartly-dressed as ever.

encore

When an audience has really enjoyed a performance and want to hear more, they clap and shout 'encore' (the French word for 'again').

Fauré, Gabriel

(1845–1924)

Fauré was a French composer and teacher. His quiet genius is shown in his beautiful songs and **chamber music**.

Fauré's best-known work is his gentle and moving *Requiem*, which he wrote in memory of his mother.

Colourful costumes, clicking castanets and stamping and shouting are all part of the excitement of flamenco.

film music

At the beginning of the 20th century the first films ('silent' films) just had pictures, with no sound. So in each cinema a pianist or cinema organist played live music to fit the action (and also to cover the noise of the film projectors!). In the 1930s films started to include sound, and composers began to write special background music to create more atmosphere and increase suspense. Film composers have to write music on demand to suit any mood, timed exactly to fit the scene on the screen.

fingering

Fingering is deciding which finger plays which note when playing a keyboard, string or woodwind instrument.

Fitzgerald, Ella

(1918–1996)

Ella Fitzgerald was one of the greatest American jazz singers. She was an orphan, and at 16 won first prize in a talent competition. Her career started when a bandleader in the audience adopted her. Ella Fitzgerald's crystal-clear voice and polished style were ideal for slow love songs, and she was also a brilliant **scat** singer.

Ella Fitzgerald's recordings of great American songs are classics. Listen to anything from the *Gershwin Songbook*.

flamenco

Flamenco is a vivid and rhythmic type of Spanish music. It developed from the gypsy and Arab music of southern Spain. The guitar is the most important flamenco instrument, and it accompanies energetic flamenco singing and dancing.

folk music

Every country has its own traditional music, which is called folk music ('folk' means 'of the people'). It often consists of the music used in the daily lives of ordinary people, such as nursery rhymes, work songs and dance tunes. Often folk music has been passed on from one person to another over centuries, and no one knows who composed it. Sometimes folk music and folk songs accompany folk dancing, like English morris dancing, or traditional folk events like Japanese Noh plays.

Different types of tin whistle are popular folk instruments all over the world.

fugue

A fugue is a piece entirely based on one short tune. First the tune is played or sung by itself. Then one by one other voices or instruments enter with it in turn. They combine with each other and develop it in new ways. Sometimes the tune appears upside down, backwards, slowed down or speeded up.

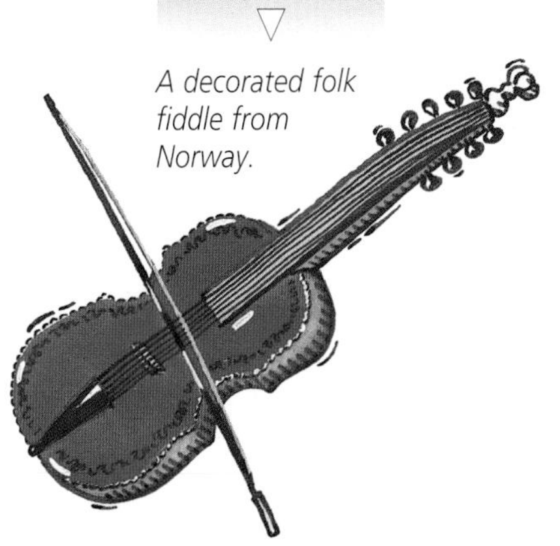

A decorated folk fiddle from Norway.

The piano accordion is a reed instrument that is played by a keyboard. The player squeezes the instrument to blow air through the reeds.

The cimbalom, a Hungarian folk instrument, has strings struck with small hammers.

gamelan

A gamelan is a type of orchestra from South-East Asia. It has about 40 members. Most of them play beautifully decorated metallophones and xylophones. There are also drums, gongs and a few wind and string instruments. Gamelan music often consists of improvisations on scales of five notes (pentatonic scales).

In Indonesia, many villages have their own gamelan. It often accompanies puppet plays or operas.

Gershwin, George

(1898–1937)

George Gershwin was America's greatest songwriter. He once said that he had more tunes in his head than he could write down in a lifetime! He composed some of the world's most memorable songs, writing catchy tunes to fit clever and funny words by his brother Ira. Gershwin was the first composer to combine classical styles with jazz, especially in his famous *Rhapsody in Blue* for piano and orchestra. He died of a brain tumour, tragically young at the age of 39.

Famous songs by the Gershwin brothers include 'I Got Rhythm', 'Summertime' and 'Let's Fall in Love'.

gig

A gig is the nickname that players use for any kind of performance or concert. It can be a jazz or pop group playing in a pub, or an orchestra playing in a concert hall.

Gilbert and Sullivan

William Gilbert (1836–1911) and Sir Arthur Sullivan (1842–1900) were an English partnership of author and composer. Gilbert's amusing words and Sullivan's tuneful music made their comic operas very popular in Victorian England. The best-known are *The Mikado*, *HMS Pinafore*, and *The Pirates of Penzance*. The pair frequently quarrelled, and Sullivan would really rather have been famous for his serious music instead.

glissando

A glissando is a sliding sound that moves smoothly up or down between notes. On the piano or harp, you slide a finger quickly across all the keys or strings.

gospel music

Gospel is a joyful and enthusiastic type of black American church music. Gospel singing is highly emotional, and combines the heartfelt religious feelings of **spirituals** with jazzy rhythms.

graphic score

A graphic score is a way of writing down music so that it looks like a picture. Graphic scores use shapes, symbols or patterns rather than the usual system of written music, or notation.

Gregorian chant is the oldest music of the Christian Church. It was the first music ever to be written down and has its own special system of musical symbols which is still in use today, over 1,000 years later.

Gregorian chant

Gregorian chant is another name for plainsong. It is a simple unaccompanied melody that is usually sung by monks or nuns. It has religious words, often from the Catholic **mass**, and it gently follows their rhythm.

grunge

Grunge is a style of rock music that started in Seattle, USA in the late 1980s. Grunge groups wore baggy clothes from second-hand shops and sang angry songs about life. The most famous grunge group was Nirvana, whose lead singer, Kurt Cobain, stunned his fans by committing suicide in 1994.

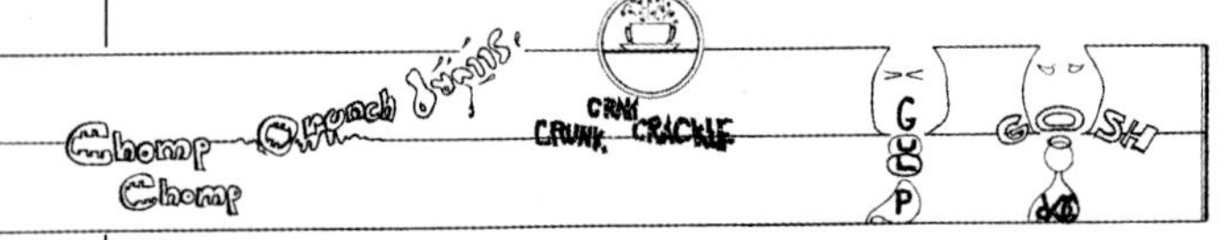

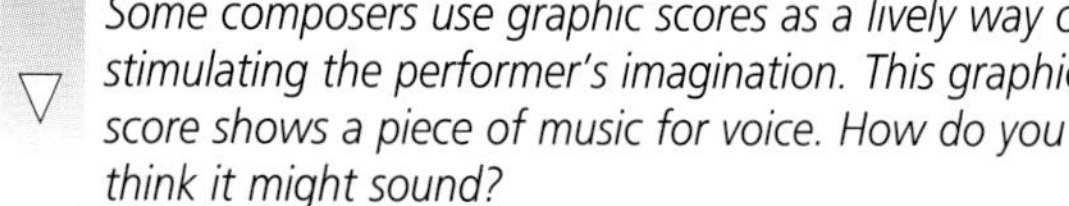

Some composers use graphic scores as a lively way of stimulating the performer's imagination. This graphic score shows a piece of music for voice. How do you think it might sound?

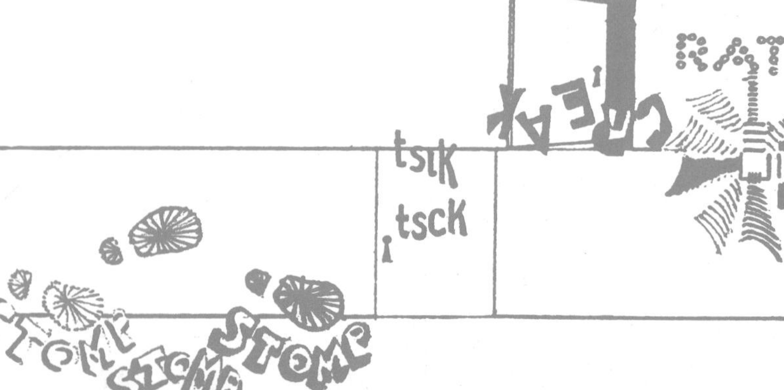

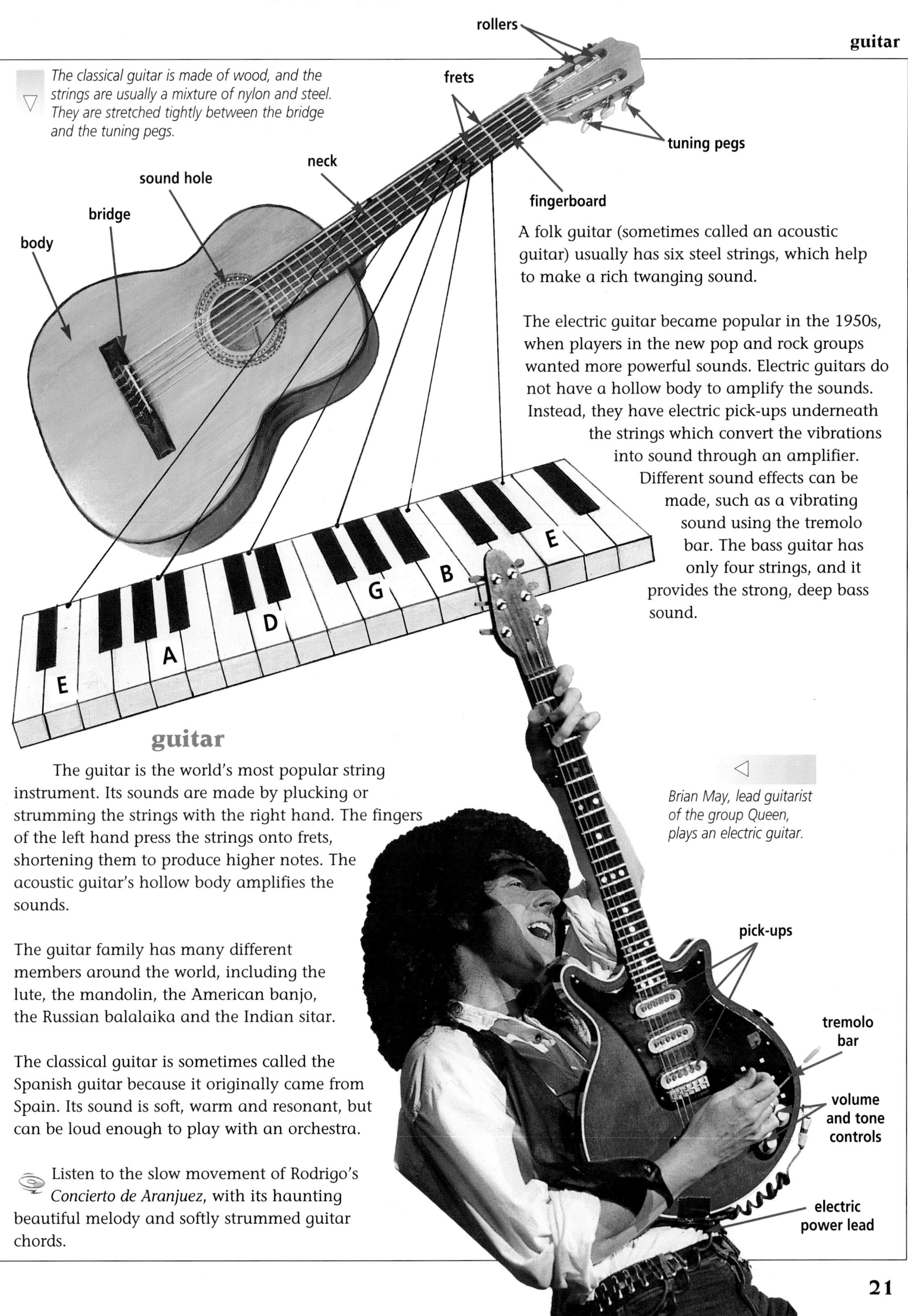

The classical guitar is made of wood, and the strings are usually a mixture of nylon and steel. They are stretched tightly between the bridge and the tuning pegs.

Brian May, lead guitarist of the group Queen, plays an electric guitar.

guitar

The guitar is the world's most popular string instrument. Its sounds are made by plucking or strumming the strings with the right hand. The fingers of the left hand press the strings onto frets, shortening them to produce higher notes. The acoustic guitar's hollow body amplifies the sounds.

The guitar family has many different members around the world, including the lute, the mandolin, the American banjo, the Russian balalaika and the Indian sitar.

The classical guitar is sometimes called the Spanish guitar because it originally came from Spain. Its sound is soft, warm and resonant, but can be loud enough to play with an orchestra.

Listen to the slow movement of Rodrigo's *Concierto de Aranjuez*, with its hauntingly beautiful melody and softly strummed guitar chords.

A folk guitar (sometimes called an acoustic guitar) usually has six steel strings, which help to make a rich twanging sound.

The electric guitar became popular in the 1950s, when players in the new pop and rock groups wanted more powerful sounds. Electric guitars do not have a hollow body to amplify the sounds. Instead, they have electric pick-ups underneath the strings which convert the vibrations into sound through an amplifier. Different sound effects can be made, such as a vibrating sound using the tremolo bar. The bass guitar has only four strings, and it provides the strong, deep bass sound.

H

Haydn, Franz Joseph

(1732–1809)

Haydn was an Austrian composer. He worked as a musician for the noble Esterházy family, composing for their private opera house and chapel. Haydn produced a huge amount of music, but his endless musical imagination invented something new and original in almost every piece. On visits to England, Haydn was impressed by Handel's oratorios, and later wrote a marvellous one of his own about the creation of the world.

Haydn loved musical jokes. In the slow movement of his *Surprise* Symphony he put in a sudden loud chord to wake the audience up.

Listen to the opening of *The Creation*. It depicts the universe in darkness and then gloriously transformed by the creation of light.

Handel wrote his Fireworks Music *to accompany this magnificent firework display in 1749. 12, 000 people turned out for the rehearsal, causing a three-hour traffic jam on London Bridge.*

Handel, George Frideric

(1685–1759)

Handel was one of the greatest composers of **baroque music**. He was born in Germany, but spent most of his life in England. He was a great organist and harpsichordist, but he became most famous as a composer of operas. Many of these were written for his own opera company. When that collapsed he turned instead to composing oratorio, a kind of religious opera performed in churches. Handel's greatest work, the **oratorio** *Messiah*, is packed with lively tunes and dramatic moments like the 'Hallelujah' Chorus.

Try Handel's *Water Music,* which was written for a royal picnic on the river Thames.

harmony

Harmony is the combination of notes together in chords. When you whistle or sing a tune, there is no harmony. But if you start inventing chords on the piano to go with the tune, then you are harmonizing it. Harmony can make a tune more interesting and change its character.

heavy metal

Heavy metal is a very loud type of rock music. The sound is amplified (made louder), so that the drums and guitars thunder out a deafening beat. Fans of heavy metal are sometimes called 'headbangers' because of the way they dance and their love of a painfully high noise level.

Jimmy Page from the famous heavy metal group Led Zeppelin.

Holiday, Billie

(1915–1959)

Billie Holiday was a jazz singer whose real name was Eleanora Gough McKay. She started singing in New York jazz clubs at the age of just 15. She had a difficult and unhappy personal life, and drug addiction led to her tragically early death.

Billie Holiday had a husky voice that made her blues singing very personal and emotional.

'Strange Fruit' is Billie Holiday's most remarkable song. It has disturbing and sinister words about racism in the American Deep South.

Holst, Gustav

(1874–1934)

Holst was an English composer. His music is very original, inspired by influences as different as Hinduism and English folk song. Holst's most famous work is *The Planets*, for large orchestra and a wordless women's choir. Each movement is a vivid picture of the magical forces of the planets in our solar system.

'Mars, the Bringer of War' and 'Neptune, the Mystic' from *The Planets*.

house music

House music developed in the late 1980s and is named after the Warehouse Club in Chicago, USA. It uses short extracts (samples) of sound or music – anything from bits of other music to news items. They are remixed and re-recorded over a fast, repetitive backing rhythm, produced by a synthesizer.

hymn

A hymn is a religious song used during worship. The Rig-Veda hymns of the Hindu religion are over 3,000 years old. Christian hymns are sung by church congregations, usually accompanied by the organ. They were written with strong, simple tunes so that people would remember the words and learn about religion from them. Modern Christian hymns are written in a pop style and accompanied by guitars and other instruments.

impromptu

An impromptu is a short, cheerful piano piece.

As well as playing hymns, organists often have to improvise to fill in gaps in the church service, especially when a bride is late arriving for her wedding!

improvisation

Improvisation is making up music as you are playing or singing. When you improvise, every performance is different. You may have decided beforehand that you want your piece to be based on certain chords or to follow a particular plan, but there is nothing written down to follow. **Jazz** often consists of improvisations on popular tunes. Improvisation is also important in **folk music** and Indian classical music.

Instru

Everybody owns at least one instrument – their voice! The very earliest music was probably singing. The first instruments were made from wood, shells or bone, and were blown, shaken or tapped. Now there are hundreds of different instruments that are played throughout the world, but they can all be grouped into families by how they make their different sounds.

Wind Instruments

Wind instruments produce sound by vibrating a column of air inside a tube. Changing the length of the tube produces different notes. The longer the tube, the deeper the note.

woodwind family

Woodwind instruments were originally made of wood. They are really just tubes with holes in. Opening and closing the holes with your fingers or with keys alters the length of the tube. Woodwind players make sounds either by blowing across an edge or by blowing a **reed** to make it vibrate. The clarinet and saxophone have single reeds. The oboe, cor anglais and bassoon have double reeds.
See also **recorder**.

piccolo

The piccolo is a small flute that sounds very high and shrill.

The clarinet has a rich, mellow sound. There are many concertos written for it. One of the best is by Mozart.

flute

reed goes here

The oboe makes a very plaintive sound.

reed goes here

Scottish bagpipes

There are many different types of bagpipes. These are Scottish bagpipes played by an army pipe major.

The saxophone was invented in 1846 and named after its inventor, Adolphe Sax.

The bassoon is over 3 metres in length, but is folded back on itself to make it easier to hold.

brass family

Brass instruments are long metal tubes, coiled round to make them easier to hold. Brass players squeeze their lips across a mouthpiece and blow to make them vibrate. Different notes are produced by different lip shapes and by changing the length of the tube with a slide on the trombone or with valves (which shut off sections of the tube) on the other instruments.

trombone

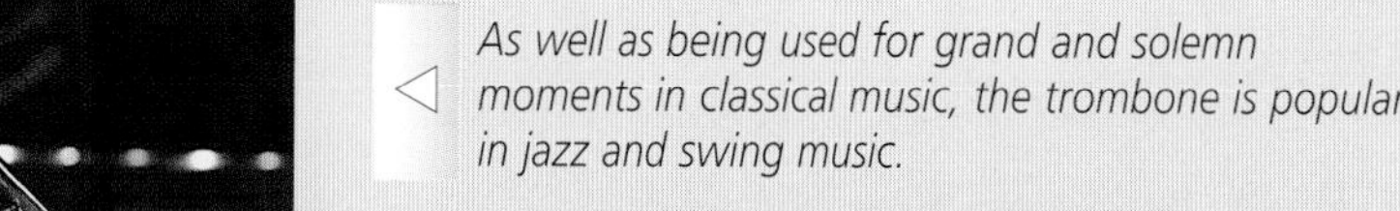

As well as being used for grand and solemn moments in classical music, the trombone is popular in jazz and swing music.

keyboard family

Keyboard instruments all have keys of some sort, which are pressed down to play each note. The most important keyboard instrument is the **piano**.

The harpsichord was the forerunner of the piano. Its strings are plucked with a plectrum, made from a small piece of metal, leather or quill (the hard, white part at the end of a feather).

The organ has several different keyboards as well as a pedal keyboard played by the feet. Each keyboard and the pedal-board is linked to a number of sets of pipes, with their own distinct sounds. Pressing a key on the organ allows air from a bellows to blow through the pipes for that note. Sound is produced in the same way as for wind instruments.

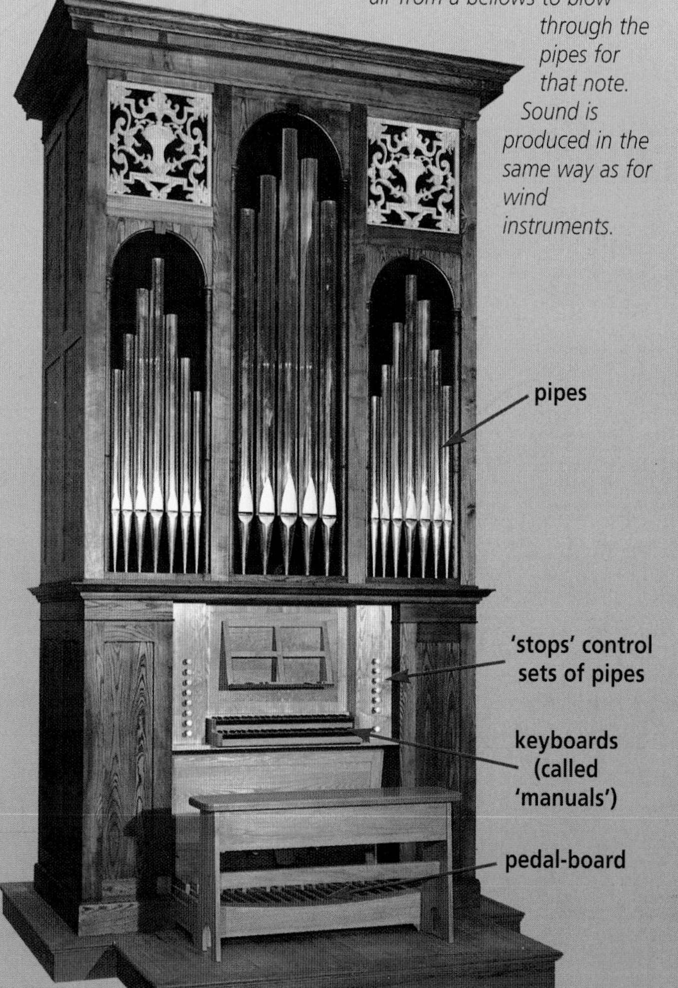

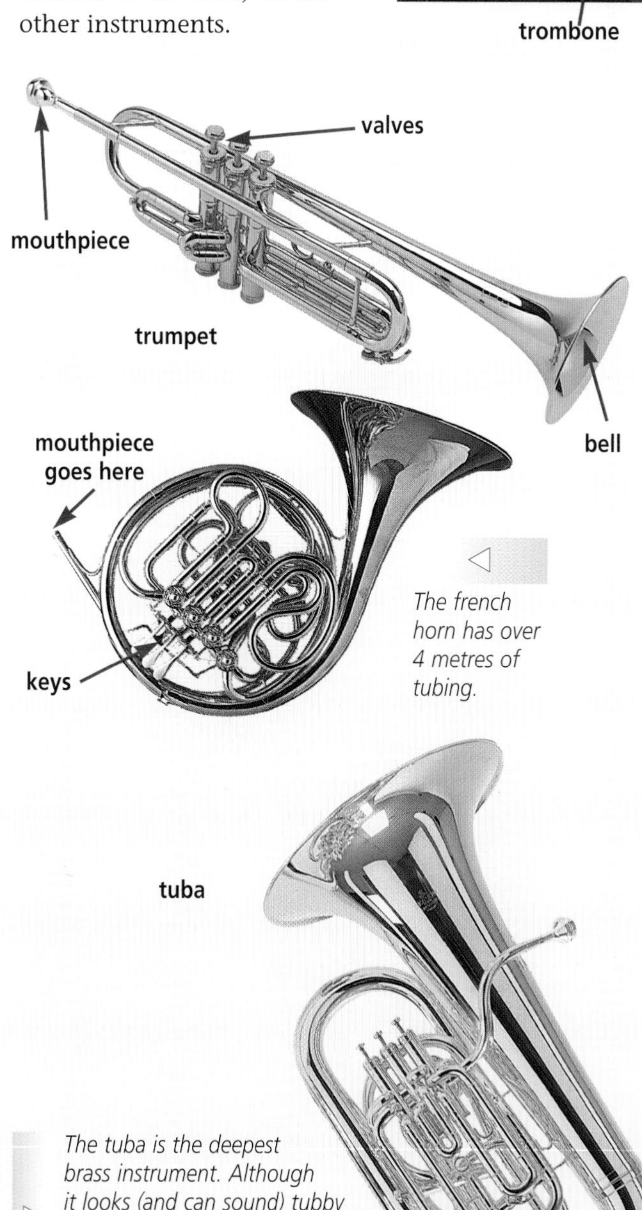

The french horn has over 4 metres of tubing.

The tuba is the deepest brass instrument. Although it looks (and can sound) tubby and clumsy, a piece like Vaughan William's Tuba Concerto shows off its best qualities.

More instruments. . . . . .

Instruments

String family

String instruments have tightly stretched strings that vibrate to produce sound. The shorter the string, the higher the note. On all string instruments except the harp the player shortens the strings by pressing them down onto a fingerboard with one hand. Meanwhile, the other hand produces the sound by bowing, plucking or strumming the strings. There are two sorts of string instruments: those that are *bowed* and those that are *plucked.*

▷ *The cello is gripped between the player's knees and has a spike to stop it slipping.*

spike

PLUCKED instruments are played by plucking and strumming (or occasionally hitting) the strings. Sometimes this is done with a small piece of hard material called a plectrum, instead of with the fingers. The most common plucked string instruments are the different types of **guitar**.

◁ *The violin and viola are held between the player's chin and shoulder.*

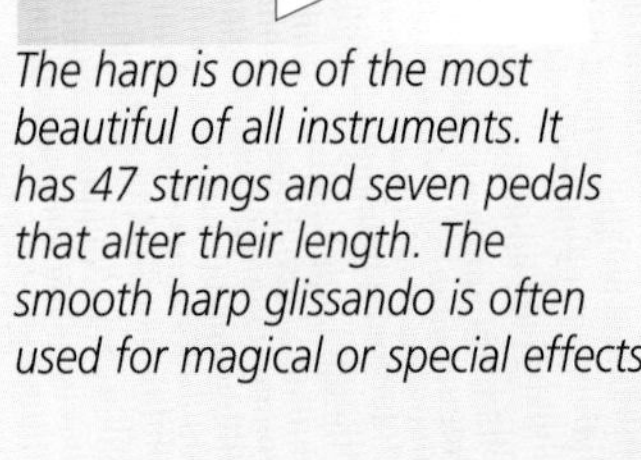

▷ *The harp is one of the most beautiful of all instruments. It has 47 strings and seven pedals that alter their length. The smooth harp glissando is often used for magical or special effects.*

BOWED instruments are played by stroking the strings with a bow, a piece of wood with a bunch of hair stretched tightly between its ends.

The double bass is the largest and deepest string instrument. ▷

△ *The Indian sitar has about 20 metal strings, four of which are plucked to create the melody.*

. . . . . . *More instruments*

Percussion family

Percussion instruments are the simplest instruments of all. You play most percussion instruments by striking them. The sound produced depends on what the instrument is made of, what you strike it with, and how you strike it.

There are hundreds of different percussion instruments, and different regions of the world have their own types of instruments, often made from local materials.

TUNED percussion instruments have notes tuned to a definite **pitch**, and are played with different types of beaters. They include the glockenspiel, **xylophone**, **steel band**, **gamelan**, cow bells, wood blocks, and kettledrums.

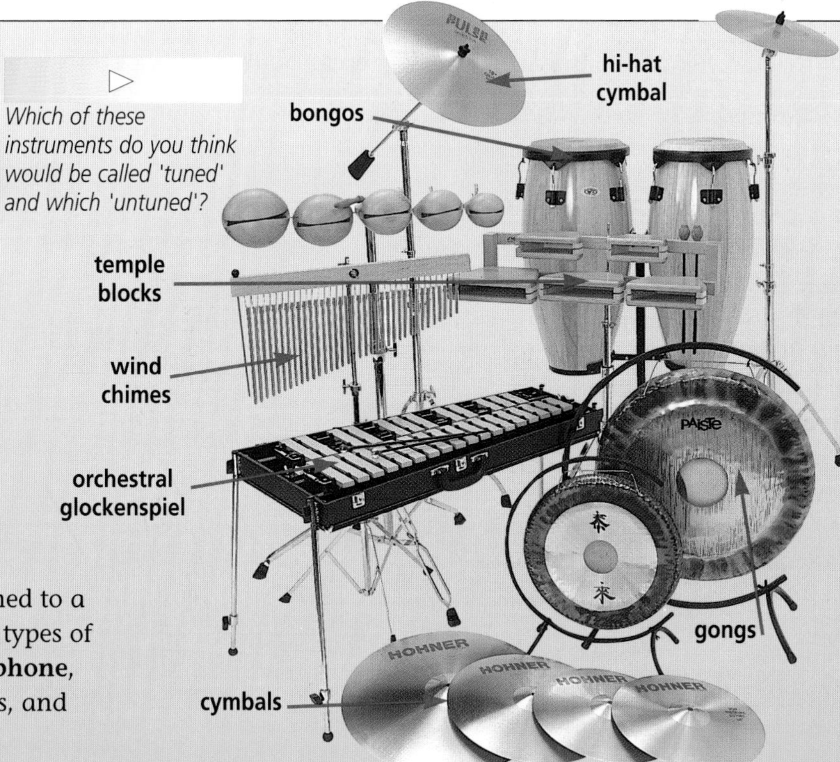

▷ *Which of these instruments do you think would be called 'tuned' and which 'untuned'?*

◁ *The kettledrums used in a modern symphony orchestra are called the timpani. They can be tuned to different notes by using a pedal that alters the tension of the plastic drum surface.*

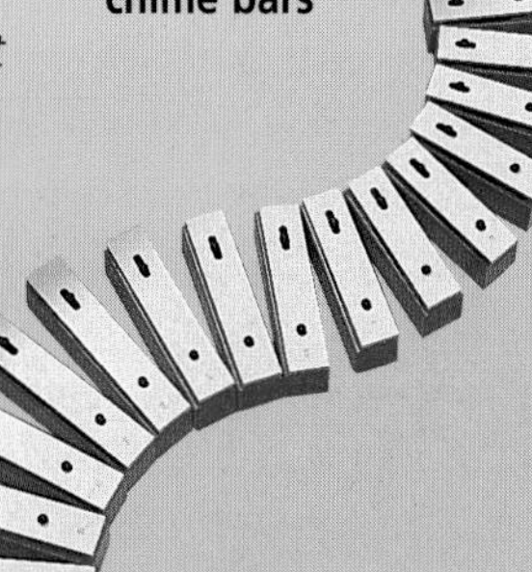

UNTUNED percussion instruments produce sounds of no fixed pitch, and usually make their sounds by being shaken, struck, or scraped. They include cymbals, maracas and afuches, wind chimes, bells, castanets, triangles, gongs, whistles and many kinds of drums.

▷ *Afuches are also known as cabasas.*

△ *The drum kit often accompanies pop and jazz groups. One player is able to play several different drums and cymbals, and other instruments can be kept within reach.*

jazz

Jazz is a style of popular music. Jazz musicians usually make up the music as they go along by **improvising** on popular tunes. There are many different sorts of jazz, both played and sung. But you can usually spot jazz by its relaxed style and strong, catchy rhythms.

The British jazz saxophone player, Courtney Pine. He first played in reggae bands, which has influenced his jazz playing.

Jazz developed around 1900 from black American music like **ragtime** and **blues**. It began in New Orleans, USA, where the bands playing at funerals or street parties improvised on tunes like 'When the saints go marching in', making them more lively by jazzing them up.

The first jazz musicians usually played by ear (without written music). Early jazz bands consisted of trumpet, clarinet and trombone, with foot-tapping rhythms kept going by the piano, banjo, double bass and drums. Their music was relaxed and easygoing. The trumpeter Louis Armstrong was the most famous player of this kind of music, which is called traditional jazz. Later, the saxophone became an important jazz instrument.

In the 1940s, some jazz musicians wanted to do something new and different, so they invented modern jazz (called 'bebop'). It is more complicated than traditional jazz or swing, and is intended for serious listening.

See also Louis **Armstrong**, **blues**, **boogie-woogie**, Duke **Ellington**, Ella **Fitzgerald**, Billie **Holiday**, **improvisation**, Glen **Miller**, **ragtime**, **rhythm 'n' blues**, **scat**, **swing**.

In the 1930s, big bands like Duke Ellington's became popular, playing written-down dance music called 'swing'.

juke box

A juke box is a coin-in-the-slot machine for playing music. In the 1950s you could find them in almost every pub and coffee bar.

karaoke

Karaoke was invented by the Japanese in the 1980s and has become popular all over the world. A karaoke machine plays recordings of pop songs without the voice of the singer. Anyone who takes the microphone can pretend to be a pop star by singing along.

key

The key of a piece of music is named after the **scale** it uses. For example, music using the **scale** of G is said to be 'in the key of G'. A 'key signature' is the group of sharps or flats that comes at the beginning of each line of written music, to remind you to play them.
See also **major**.

key signature of G major (one sharp, F#)

The tune 'God Save the Queen' in the key of G major. Notice how it begins and ends on the 'keynote' G.

keyboard

The keyboard is the part of a piano, synthesizer, harpsichord or organ that has the notes you play (the keys). In pop music, keyboards are any electronic keyboard instruments that are used, such as synthesizers or electric pianos.
See also **instruments** (keyboard family).

L

libretto

The libretto is another name for the words of an opera or musical. Reading the libretto beforehand will help you understand what happens on stage.

Liszt, Franz

(1811–1886)

Liszt was a Hungarian composer. He was a piano **virtuoso** from the age of 11, and most of his music was written to show off his brilliant playing. Liszt was a handsome young man, and his dashing image and magnetic personality made him an international celebrity. Despite some scandalous love affairs in his younger days, in his fifties he became a priest.

Imagine the thrilling effect of Liszt's playing by listening to his *Hungarian Rhapsody No. 1*. It is based on Hungarian gypsy music.

Lloyd Webber, Andrew

(born 1948)

Andrew Lloyd Webber is an English composer who is famous for his hugely successful musicals. He started composing when he was six, helped by his father. His first big hit was a school rock musical, *Joseph and the Amazing Technicolor Dreamcoat*. It was followed by *Jesus Christ Superstar, Evita, Cats, Starlight Express* and *The Phantom of the Opera. Cats* is the longest running musical in the history of the theatre. See also **musicals**.

lullaby

A lullaby is a gentle song that is sung to help a child go to sleep, like 'Rock-a-bye Baby'.

lyrics

The words of pop and show songs are called their lyrics.

◁ *A cartoon showing Liszt's extraordinary personality; a mixture of saintly priest and keyboard wizard.*

▽ *The phantom of the opera, from Andrew Lloyd Webber's musical of the same name.*

madrigal

A madrigal is an unaccompanied song for several voices. Most English madrigals were composed in Elizabethan times, when they were a popular entertainment to sing at home with friends or family.

Mahler, Gustav

(1860–1911)

Mahler was an Austrian composer. In his lifetime he was more famous as a brilliant conductor, and he could only concentrate on composing during his holidays from conducting opera.

Mahler is best known for his nine symphonies. They need a huge orchestra, often with voices, and are very long and powerful. Mahler wanted them to represent all aspects of his intense life, and they are full of contrasting moods: tortured and tender, peaceful and panic-stricken, sinister and comic.

An American marching club, led by a sousaphone player.

march

A march is a piece with a strong beat written to help soldiers (or other marchers) keep in step.

The American composer John Philip Sousa wrote over 100 marches, and is known as 'The March King'. A marching-band instrument, the sousaphone, was named after him.
See also **military band**.

major

Scales and **keys** in western music come in two main types called major and minor. Major keys and scales sound more cheerful. Composers use them for happy, bright or contented music. Minor keys and scales are used for serious, sad or scary music.

Find a keyboard and try playing these two scales. Which sounds sadder?

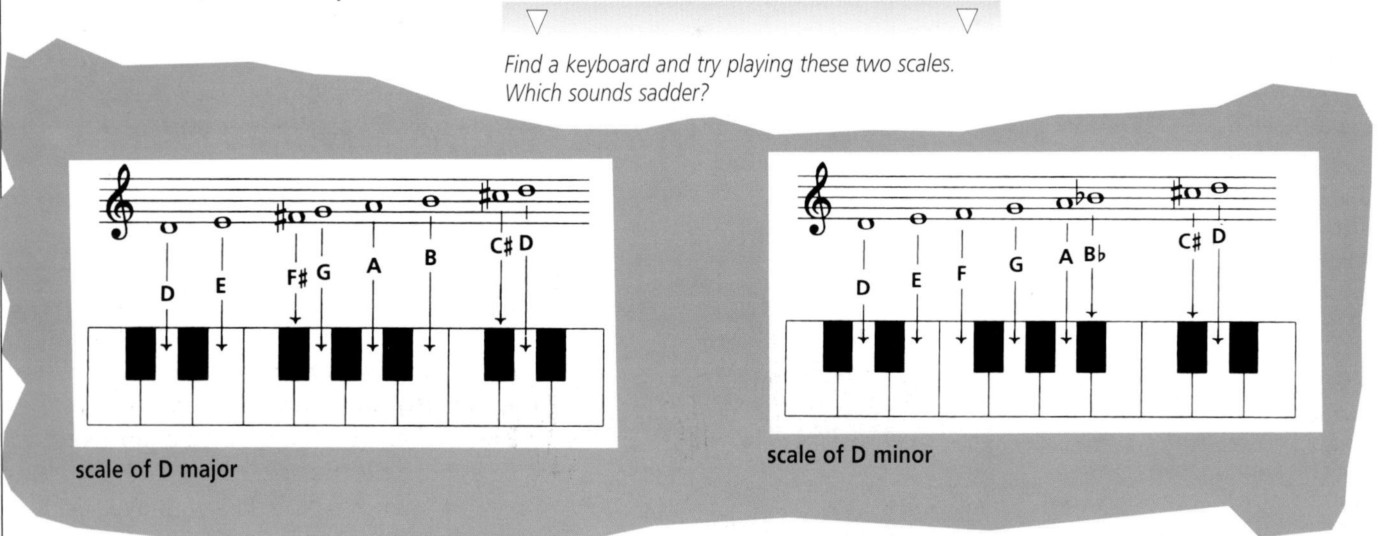

mass

The mass is the main service of the Roman Catholic Church, and it is often set to music. Its text was originally in Latin, though nowadays you hear it in English too. The mass comes in five contrasting sections, or movements. Many composers have composed masses, in styles ranging from **Gregorian chant** to **flamenco**.
See also **religious music**, **requiem**.

For two unusual and contrasting masses, try Paco Peña's *Missa flamenca* ('Flamenco mass') and Britten's *Missa brevis* ('Short Mass') for boys' voices and organ.

melody

Melody is another word for tune. A melody is a series of musical notes that you can recognize and remember. It may be part of a longer piece of music, or may stand on its own. If you compare an Indian **raga** or a Chinese folk melody with a hit pop song, it is clear that the idea of a good tune is completely different in different parts of the world.

Messiaen spent a lot of time writing down birdsongs, and his compositions such as Oiseaux Exotiques (Exotic birds) often contain musical impressions of them.

Mendelssohn, Felix

(1809–1847)

Mendelssohn was a German composer. He was a brilliant pianist at the age of nine, and composed some of his best music before he was 20. Mendelssohn loved to travel. He visited Scotland and Italy, and was inspired by the beautiful scenery to write his popular 'Scottish' and 'Italian' Symphonies. He died from overwork, aged only 38.

The thrilling first movement of Mendelssohn's String Octet bubbles over with talent and energy. He wrote it when he was just 16!

Two sorts of metronome: the mechanical one (top) is wound up and ticks like a clock; the more modern electronic one (bottom) beeps or flashes a light.

Messiaen, Olivier

(1908–1992)

Messiaen was a French composer and organist. His music is very mysterious and religious. It is full of weird sounds and colourful percussion instruments.

Try 'Joie du Sang des Étoiles' ('The Joy in the blood of the Stars') from *Turangalîla-symphonie.* It features an unusual electronic instrument called the ondes-martenot.

metronome

A metronome is a machine that indicates the right speed for a piece of music. It gives you a steady **beat**, either by a clicking sound or by a flashing light. You can set it to give a different number of beats per minute.

MIDI

MIDI stands for Musical Instrument Digital Interface. A MIDI is a set of electronic circuits that cleverly links **electronic instruments**, computers and **samplers** together. When you compose on a keyboard you can have the music automatically displayed on a computer screen, played back and printed out.

military band

A military band is a group of brass, woodwind and percussion players who perform at military occasions.

Sometimes military bands march as they play, with the big bass drum strapped to the front of a strong soldier.

Miller, Glen

(1904–1944)

Glen Miller was an American jazz-band leader and trombone player. Hits like 'Chattanooga choo-choo' and 'Moonlight Serenade' made the Glen Miller Orchestra the most popular **big band** in the United States. During the Second World War Miller led the American Airforce Band in Europe. While on a flight from Paris to London, his plane disappeared and no trace of it has ever been found.

minimalist music

Minimalist music is often very repetitive and hypnotic. It is built up from the bare minimum of musical material. Minimalist composers use tiny bits of tune and simple chords. They repeat them again and again, changing them gradually over long periods of time. The most famous minimalist composers are the Americans Philip Glass (born 1936) and Steve Reich (born 1937).

minor

See **major**.

minuet

A minuet is a graceful dance. It was popular in Europe during the 17th and 18th centuries, and was sometimes used for the third movement of **symphonies** and **sonatas**.

Try the Minuet from Mozart's *Eine Kleine Nachtmusik* ('A Little Night Music').

Monteverdi, Claudio

(1567–1643)

Monteverdi was an Italian composer and one of the inventors of **opera**. He worked for the Duke of Mantua, for whom he wrote **madrigals** and his first opera *Orfeo,* about Orpheus in the underworld. His fame spread and in 1613 he took charge of music at the great cathedral of St Mark's in Venice, where he wrote magnificent music for the grand services. He wrote two more great operas, *The Return of Ulysses* and *The Coronation of Poppea.*

The first two movements of Monteverdi's *Vespers* give us a sense of the splendid music at St Mark's cathedral.

movement

A long musical piece is often divided into several separate sections called movements. Each one is self-contained and usually has a different character to provide variety and contrast.

musicals

Musicals (or shows) are musical plays which have a mixture of acting, singing and dancing. The music is popular in style, and unlike **opera** the characters often speak a lot as well as sing.

Musicals developed from light operas, and their plots are usually cheerful and romantic. Lavish sets, special effects and spectacular dance sequences are part of the entertainment.

Many famous musicals were produced in the United States, in theatres on a famous street called Broadway.
See also Andrew **Lloyd Webber, Rodgers and Hammerstein**.

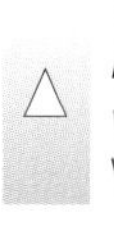
The tin man, the scarecrow, the lion and Dorothy, in the film version of the musical The Wizard of Oz.

Mozart, Wolfgang Amadeus

(1756–1791)

For many people, Mozart is the greatest composer of all. He was born in Austria and was taught music by his father, Leopold. Everyone was astonished at Mozart's outstanding talents. He found composing easy from an early age, and wrote over 600 works in his brief life. He was often short of money and had to work hard to earn a living. He died a poor man at the age of 35, and was buried in an unknown grave.

Listen to Papageno's song from *The Magic Flute* – one of Mozart's happiest and most amusing pieces.

By the age of six Mozart was a gifted harpsichord player, and his father took him and his sister Nannerl on a concert tour all over Europe.

mute

A mute is a device that muffles the sound of an instrument. On string instruments, mutes are clamps (small clips) that reduce the vibration of the strings. Mutes for brass instruments are stoppers that fit into the open end to deaden the sound.

Jazz trumpeters sometimes use their hand or a hat as a mute.

muzak

Muzak is the name used for background music played in public places like shops and restaurants.

Notation

Notation is writing music down. Music notation is a kind of code that allows other people to play your music. It uses a mixture of special signs and words to record the three main things we need to know about musical sounds.

1 How long or short are the sounds? ('rhythm')

Sounds ('notes') and silences ('rests') have different shapes which show how long they are in relation to each other.

A minim (half note) is half the length of a semibreve.

A crotchet (quarter note) is a quarter the length of a semibreve, and half the length of a minim.

Quavers (eighth notes) are an eighth of the length of a semibreve, and half the length of crotchets.

And semiquavers are half as long as quavers.

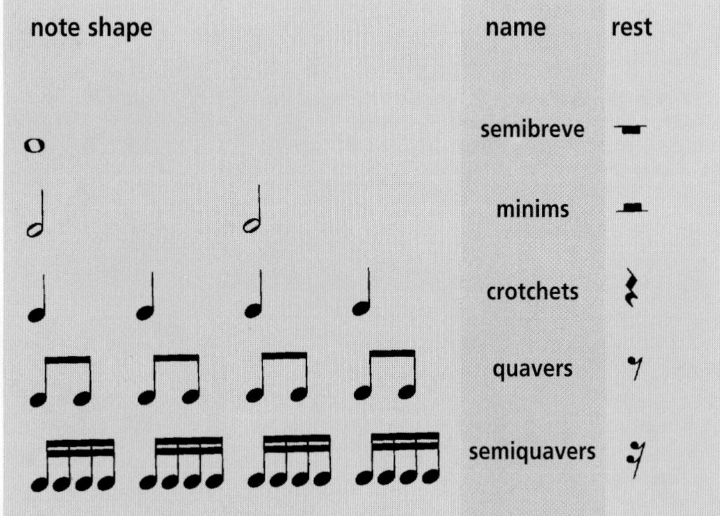

A tie between notes means that you hold the first note for the length of all the tied notes added together. Two tied crotchets last the same length as a minim.

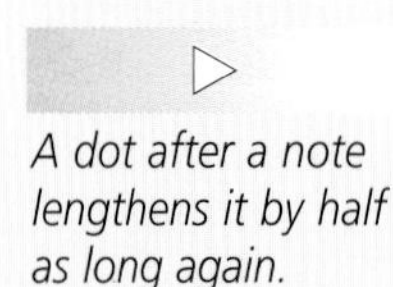

A dot after a note lengthens it by half as long again.

3 How should the music be played? ('expression')

As well as signs, composers use words to tell us how to play their music. Italian words are traditionally used, and they are often shortened to save space. They give information about mood, speed and loudness.

MOOD

Music creates moods and expresses feelings. There are as many different ways of playing as there are human feelings. Composers use lots of 'mood' words to tell performers what they want. Here are just a few:

dolce sweetly
doloroso sadly
giocoso merrily
grazioso gracefully
legato smoothly
leggiero lightly
maestoso majestically
marcato markedly
pesante heavily
scherzando playfully
semplice simply
staccato with each note very short
tranquillo calmly

SPEED ('tempo')

This speedometer shows some of the Italian words used to tell you how fast to play.

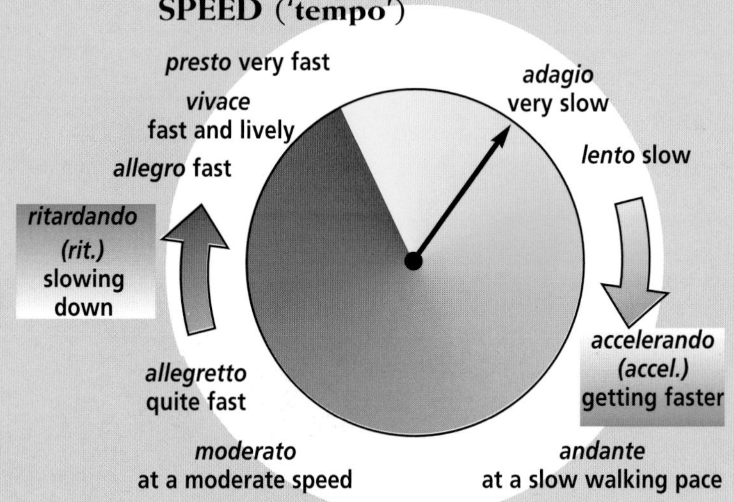

2 How high or low are the sounds? ('pitch')

Music is written on a set of five lines like a ladder, called a 'stave'. Its lines and spaces are used to represent notes. The position of a note on the stave shows how high or low the note is.

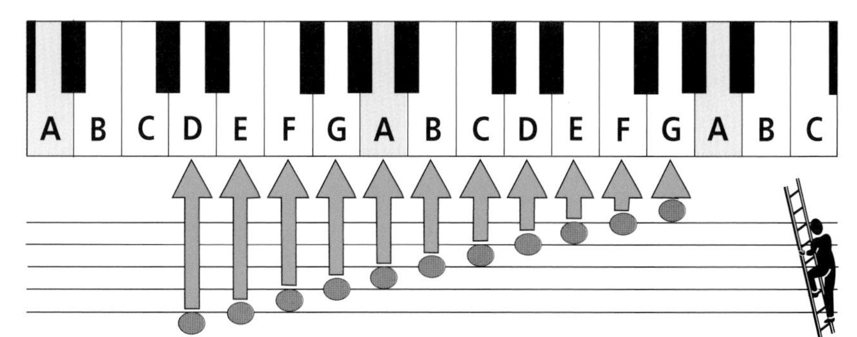

Musical notes are named after the first seven letters of the alphabet. This keyboard diagram shows where to find A. The white notes go upwards from A to G, and then repeat from A again. If you look at a real piano keyboard, the very bottom note is an A.

A *clef* is a sign used to tell you which line means which note. There are two main clefs, the *treble clef* (for higher notes) and the *bass clef* (for lower notes).

These silly sentences will help you remember the names of the lines and spaces in each clef. Read each one upwards.

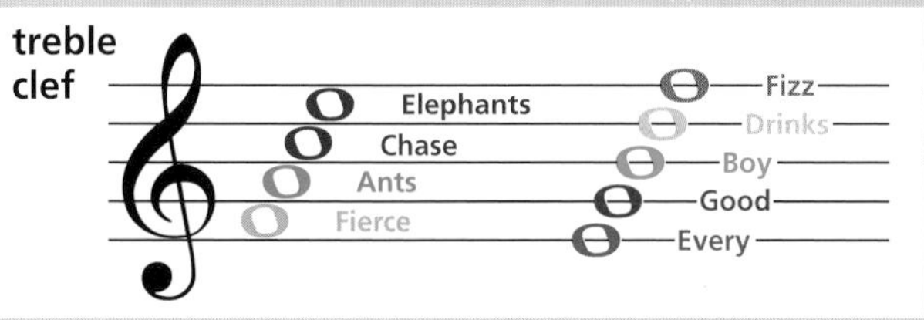

Signs called *accidentals* are written in front of notes to make them higher or lower. There are three sorts of accidentals: *sharps, flats* and *naturals* Sharps and flats are the black keys on a piano.

A flat (♭) makes a note a semitone lower.

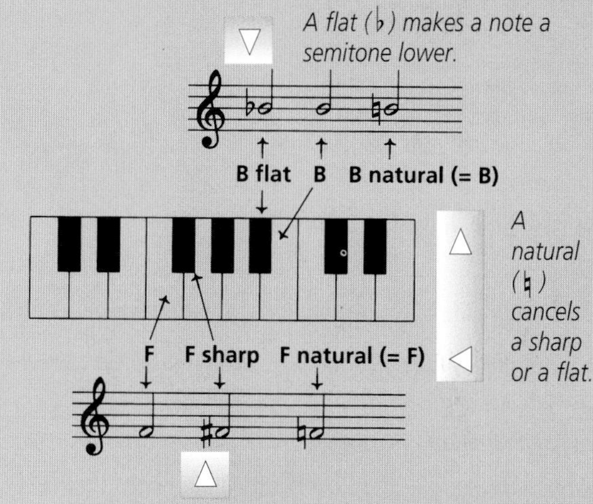

A natural (♮) cancels a sharp or a flat.

A sharp (♯) makes a note a semitone higher.

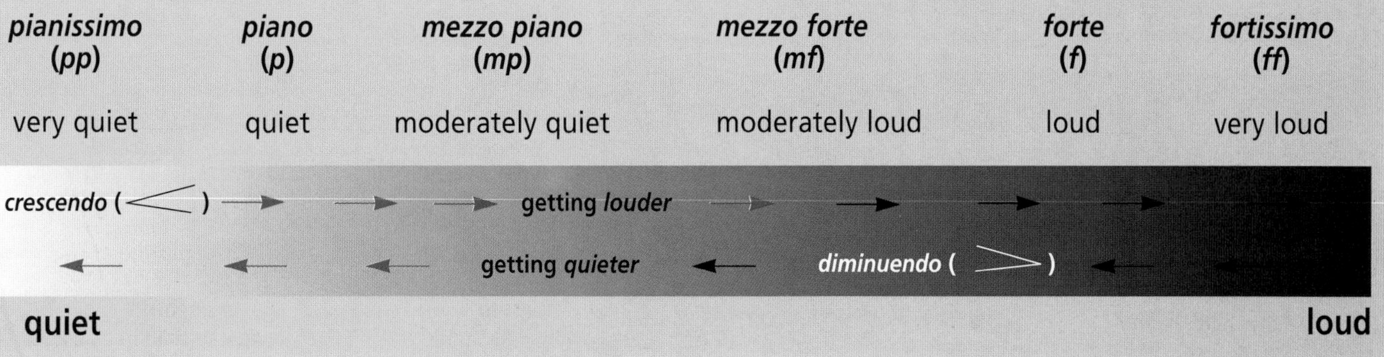

O

octave

When you go eight steps up or down the notes of a **scale**, you reach a note that is a higher or lower version of the one you started on. That note is called the octave of your starting note. Notes an octave apart have the same letter-names.

Find any A on a keyboard, and play up the eight white notes ABCDEFGA. That last A is the octave of the first one.

octet

An octet is a group of eight players, or a piece for eight instruments. The most famous octets are by Mendelssohn (eight string instruments), Beethoven (eight woodwind instruments), and Schubert (a mixture of instruments).

opera

An opera is a play that is set to music. The characters sing instead of speaking (although sometimes there is a mixture of the two).

Opera singers must be able to act as well as to sing. The best opera stars have always been famous celebrities with huge numbers of adoring fans. Often composers will write parts specially for them.

As well as good singers, opera needs a conductor, an orchestra and **chorus**, scenery, props and costumes, and lots of rehearsals. Because of this, operas are very costly to put on and tickets can be expensive. Going to the opera has always been a grand occasion, with fashionable people sometimes more interested in each other than in the music!

Opera began in Italy (which is why so many are in Italian) around 1600, with composers like **Monteverdi**. One of the earliest English operas, **Purcell's** *Dido and Aeneas*, was first performed at a girls' school in 1689. In the 18th century, opera developed into two main types. 'Opera seria' was serious, often using noble stories from legends and history. 'Opera buffa' was comic, with silly plots and lighter music. The most famous composers of these sorts of opera are **Mozart** and **Rossini**.

A scene from Verdi's grand opera Aida, which is about a love story set in ancient Egypt.

In the 19th century **Verdi** and **Wagner** developed 'grand opera'. It was often very long, with magnificent scenery, large choruses and plots including historical characters, gods and superheroes. **Wagner** invented a new sort of opera, taking control over all aspects of the music and drama, and staging his works in his own theatre. In the 20th century **Puccini**, **Strauss** and **Britten** wrote operas which treated their stories in modern, realistic ways.

19th-century light opera was called operetta. Operettas usually had sentimental, romantic stories, and the best-known ones in English are by **Gilbert and Sullivan**. In the 20th century operettas have been overtaken in popularity by **musicals**.
See also **aria**, **recitative**.

oratorio

An oratorio tells a story (often a religious one) in music. It is performed by solo singers, choir and orchestra. Oratorio was invented in Italy, and quickly became popular as an interesting way of teaching stories from the Bible. Unlike **opera**, oratorios are performed in churches or concert halls, without scenery and costumes. Oratorio was very popular in England because of the success of Handel and the enormous enthusiasm for his best-known oratorio, *Messiah*.

Four famous oratorios are Handel's *Messiah*, Haydn's *The Creation*, Elgar's *The Dream of Gerontius* and Walton's *Belshazzar's Feast*.

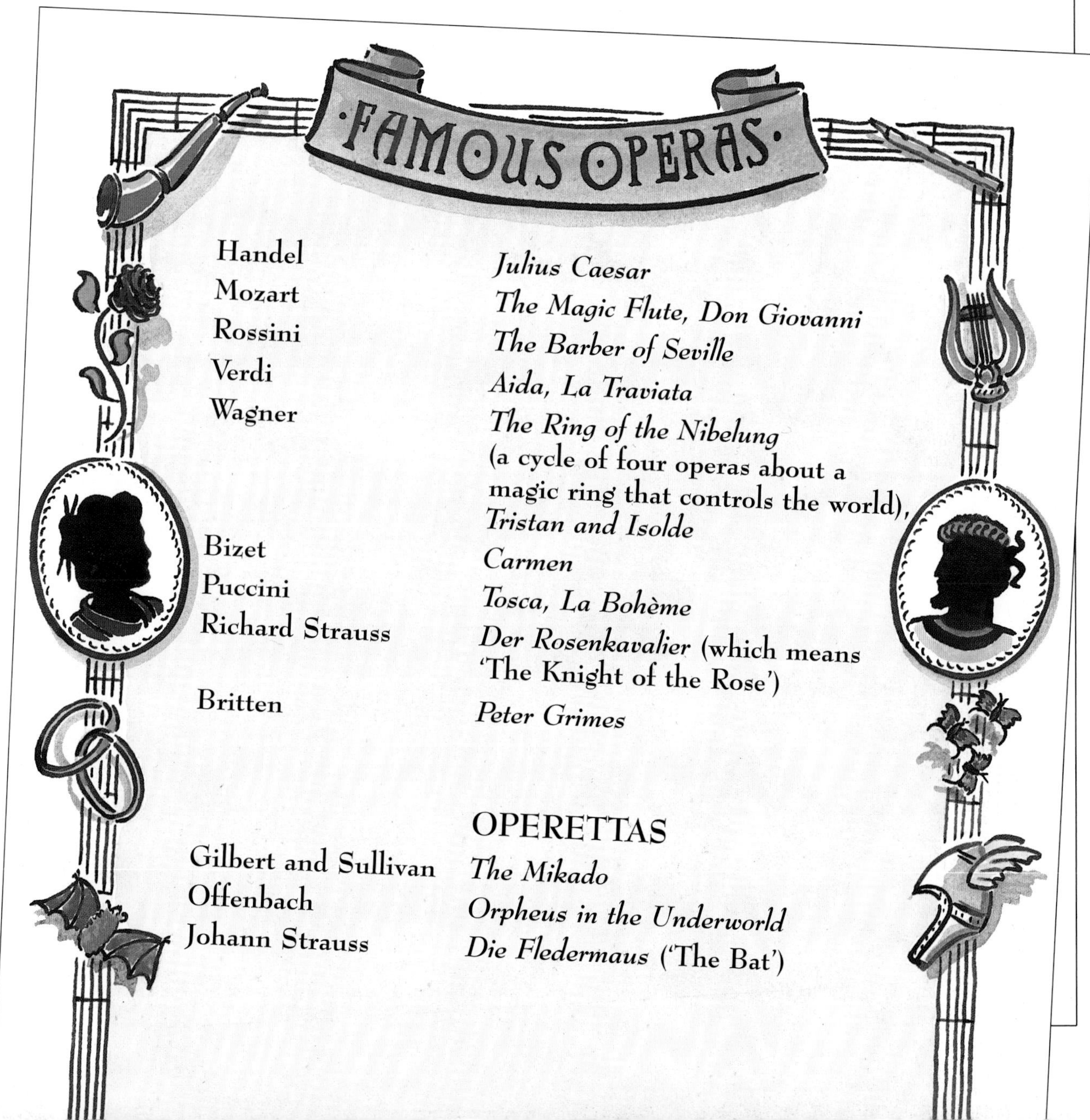

Orchestra

An orchestra is a large group of instrumentalists who play together. A modern symphony orchestra performs all sorts of western classical music (not just symphonies, despite the name). There are also **jazz** orchestras, wind orchestras, string orchestras, gamelan orchestras, and orchestras for opera, ballet, and musicals.

symphony orchestra

A **symphony** orchestra is a large group of about 80 players. It is arranged in sections, each consisting of instruments from the string, wind, brass and percussion families. Because the brass and percussion instruments are the most powerful, they are placed at the back of the orchestra to help the balance of sound.

There are a large number of string players, to produce a rich string sound. The violins are divided into two groups, called first violins and second violins. Each group plays a separate musical part.

The first violinist on the conductor's left-hand side is called the leader of the orchestra (or concert master).

As well as the usual instruments in the orchestra, composers may add others for special effects. The saxophone appears in a number of 20th-century orchestral pieces. More unusually, there are cowbells in **Mahler's** Sixth Symphony, a wind machine in **Vaughan Williams'** *Sinfonia Antarctica* ('Antarctic Symphony'), and a typewriter, steamship whistle and siren in a ballet called *Parade*, by Satie.

The London Symphony Orchestra

PERCUSSION SECTION
bass drum
cymbals
tubular bells
conductor
BRASS SECTION
horns
leader
timpani (kettle drums)
harps
STRING SECTION
first violins
second violins

history of the orchestra

The symphony orchestra as we know it today did not begin to develop until the 18th century. Before that, composers like **Monteverdi** just wrote pieces for whatever instruments happened to be at hand. In the first half of the 18th century, **Bach** and **Handel** composed for small groups consisting of flutes (or recorders), oboes, horns, trumpets, drums and string instruments.

Later in the 18th century, **Mozart** and **Haydn** composed for an orchestra that was a smaller version of today's symphony orchestra. It had about 25 players. **Beethoven's** orchestral music made new demands on the players, and his Fifth Symphony was the first symphony to use trombones.

In the 19th century the popularity of orchestral concerts grew, and large new concert halls were built to house permanent orchestras. Composers of **romantic music** (like **Berlioz**) wrote dramatic works that needed more power and greater variety of sound. The tuba, piccolo, harp, double bassoon, cor anglais and extra percussion instruments were added to the orchestra. The conductor's job became more important as the orchestra grew in size and volume. **Strauss** and **Mahler** were conductors as well as composers. Their huge works use the wonderful power and variety of the 20th-century symphony orchestra to the full.
See also **instruments**.

organ

See **instruments** (keyboard family).

ornament

An ornament is a group of a few notes that can be added to a tune to decorate it.
See also **trill**.

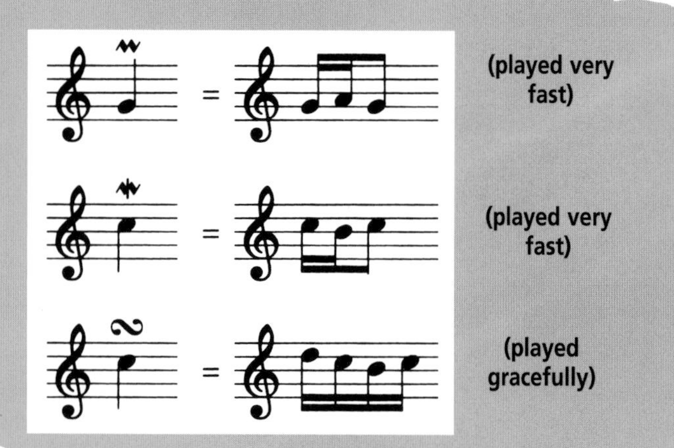

The most common ornaments are shown by special symbols that go over or under the notes in written music.

ostinato

An ostinato is a short section of tune or rhythm that is continuously repeated.

Ostinato is the Italian word for 'obstinate'. If you listen to Ravel's *Boléro* you will find out why: its ostinato rhythm starts the piece off, gets louder and louder, and refuses to budge right up to the very end.

overture

At the beginning of an **opera**, **musical** or **oratorio** you will sometimes hear a short orchestral piece called an overture. The overture was originally intended to stop the audience talking and give them a chance to settle down in their seats.

Overtures are often a selection of the best tunes from the rest of the work. Sometimes they tell a story in music.

Tchaikovsky's *1812 Overture* celebrates Napoleon's defeat in that year by the Russian army. It comes complete with cannon sounds for realistic effect.

pentatonic scale

See **scale**.

percussion instruments

See **instruments** (percussion family).

phrase

A phrase is a short section of a tune, usually short enough to be sung in one breath. In music **notation**, phrases are shown by long curved lines over the notes, like this:

piano

The piano was originally called the *pianoforte* (Italian for 'soft–loud'). You can make sounds that are loud enough to fill a large hall, or play as quietly as a whisper. The way you play is called your 'touch', and a good piano will be very sensitive to it.

① When you press a piano key, a felt-covered hammer hits the strings for that note. ② When you release the key, a piece of felt called a 'damper' rests against the strings and stops them vibrating.

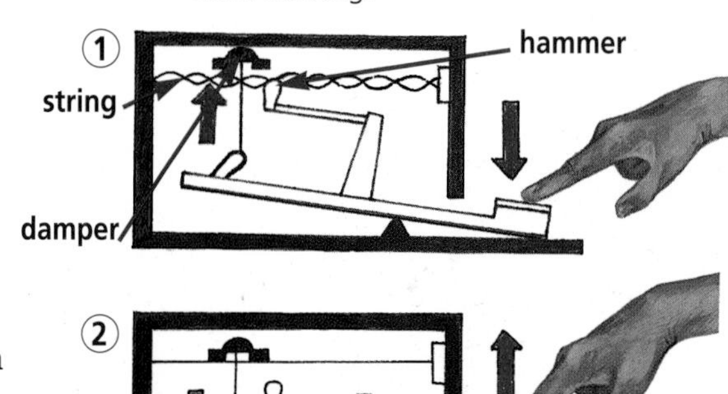

If you lift the lid of a piano and look inside, you will see that it has several strings for each note. The strings sound together, making the note louder.

A piano has two pedals. The left-hand pedal is called the 'soft pedal'. It makes the sound quieter. The right-hand pedal is called the 'sustaining pedal' (not the 'loud' pedal). It stops the dampers coming down, and this lets the sound continue after you have taken your fingers off the keys.

A 'grand piano' has its strings laid out flat, and is used in concert halls and large buildings. An 'upright piano' has its frame upright. It takes up less space and is the instrument usually found at home. As well as these, there is also the electric (or digital) piano, which produces its sound electronically. It has the advantage that you can play with headphones and avoid disturbing the neighbours.

The piano can sound powerful because it has metal strings. They are stretched very tightly across a heavy iron frame, so the hammers can hit them very hard. The total weight of these six grand pianos is about three tons, and you can imagine how loud they sound together.

pitch

The pitch of a sound is its highness or lowness. The bleeps from a microwave are high-pitched sounds, whilst rumbles of thunder are low in pitch.

In an orchestra the piccolo is the highest-pitched instrument and the double bassoon the lowest.

pizzicato

Pizzicato (usually shortened to 'pizz.') is an instruction to players of bowed string instruments like the violin. It tells them to use their finger or thumb to pluck a string. This makes a short, penetrating sound that is used for special effects.

Britten's 'Playful Pizzicato' from *Simple Symphony*

plainsong

See **Gregorian chant**.

Pop music

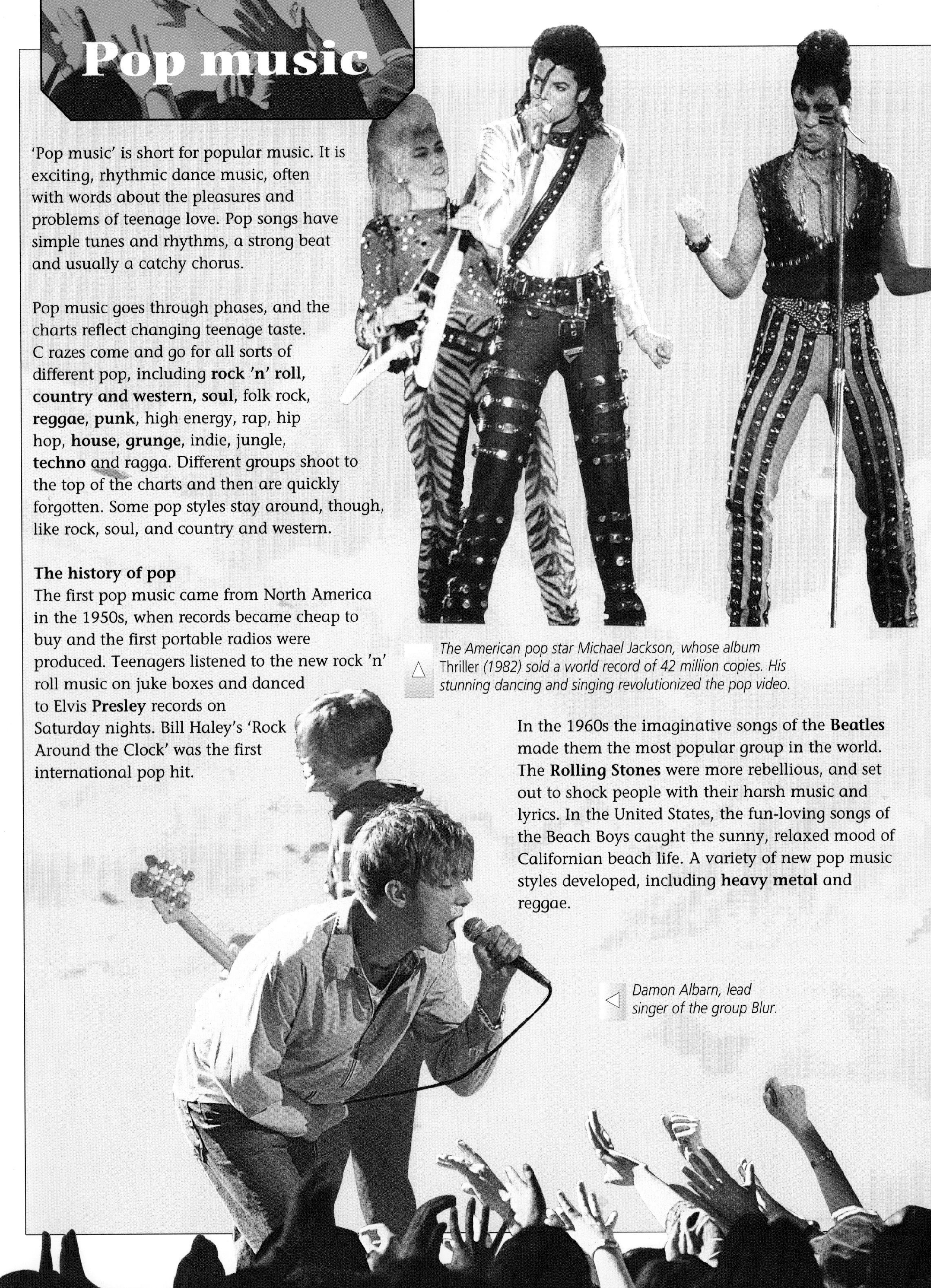

'Pop music' is short for popular music. It is exciting, rhythmic dance music, often with words about the pleasures and problems of teenage love. Pop songs have simple tunes and rhythms, a strong beat and usually a catchy chorus.

Pop music goes through phases, and the charts reflect changing teenage taste. C razes come and go for all sorts of different pop, including **rock 'n' roll, country and western**, **soul**, folk rock, **reggae**, **punk**, high energy, rap, hip hop, **house**, **grunge**, indie, jungle, **techno** and ragga. Different groups shoot to the top of the charts and then are quickly forgotten. Some pop styles stay around, though, like rock, soul, and country and western.

The history of pop

The first pop music came from North America in the 1950s, when records became cheap to buy and the first portable radios were produced. Teenagers listened to the new rock 'n' roll music on juke boxes and danced to Elvis **Presley** records on Saturday nights. Bill Haley's 'Rock Around the Clock' was the first international pop hit.

The American pop star Michael Jackson, whose album Thriller *(1982) sold a world record of 42 million copies. His stunning dancing and singing revolutionized the pop video.*

In the 1960s the imaginative songs of the **Beatles** made them the most popular group in the world. The **Rolling Stones** were more rebellious, and set out to shock people with their harsh music and lyrics. In the United States, the fun-loving songs of the Beach Boys caught the sunny, relaxed mood of Californian beach life. A variety of new pop music styles developed, including **heavy metal** and reggae.

Damon Albarn, lead singer of the group Blur.

Rock music dominated the 1970s and 80s, with groups like The Who and Pink Floyd. New technology was used by stars like Queen, David Bowie, Prince and Michael Jackson. They put on massive concerts and made videos full of stunning visual and musical effects. Styles like **punk** and **rap** rebelled against other pop music and against society in general.

1990s dance styles like **rave**, **techno** and jungle use mainly electronic sounds. New influences like **world music** are mixing with older styles, and the pop world is as vibrant and varied as ever.

Porter, Cole

(1891–1964)

Cole Porter was an American song composer. He came from a rich family who wanted him to be a lawyer. Eventually he changed to music and went on to write a string of hit songs like 'Let's Do It' and 'Who wants to be a Millionaire?'

prelude

A prelude is a short instrumental piece. Preludes are often intended to be played before something else, often a **fugue** or an **opera**. The piano preludes of composers like Chopin, Debussy and Gershwin were written as single pieces.

Bach's Prelude and Fugue in C (no. 1 from *The Well-tempered Clavier*), Chopin's 'Raindrop' Prelude.

Presley, Elvis

(1935–1977)

The first and greatest **rock 'n' roll** star was the American singer Elvis Presley. He was discovered by chance when he went to a studio to record a song for his mother's birthday. His rich voice and moody good looks led to the success of his first million-selling record, 'Heartbreak Hotel' (1956). After two years in the army, he became a film star and had a series of movie hits. Elvis sold more golden discs (million sellers) than any other artist. His early death stunned his fans and every year thousands of them still visit his home, 'Gracelands', in Memphis, Tennessee.

Try 'Blue Suede Shoes' and 'Hound Dog'.

Although he died in 1977, to his many devoted fans Elvis Presley is still 'The King'.

prima donna

A prima donna (Italian for 'first lady') is the most important female singer in an opera company. Prima donnas used to have a reputation for always wanting to be the centre of attention and behaving badly.

programme music

Programme music is instrumental music specially composed to tell a story or create the mood of a poem or picture. Composers from **Vivaldi** to Richard **Strauss** have invented all sorts of clever ways to show non-musical things in sound.

Rimsky-Korsakov's *Sheherazade* uses music to conjure up tales from the *Arabian Nights*, while each movement in Mussorgsky's *Pictures at an Exhibition* paints a picture in music.

Prokofiev, Sergey

(1891–1953)

Prokofiev was one of this century's four outstanding Russian composers, with Rachmaninov, Stravinsky and Shostakovich. He composed an opera at the age of nine, and his five piano concertos were written to show off his own amazing playing. His music is colourful, often clever and cheeky. He wrote brilliant and exciting music for ballets and films.

Peter and the Wolf, Lieutenant Kijé Suite

Proms

The Proms are a series of concerts at the Royal Albert Hall in London. 'Proms' is short for 'promenade concerts', which are concerts where some of the audience stand up and sometimes walk around. The Proms have been held each summer since 1895.

One of the most enjoyable pieces of programme music is The Sorcerer's Apprentice, *by a French composer called Paul Dukas. A magician's lazy assistant discovers a spell to make a set of broomsticks come alive and carry water for him. But he can't remember how to stop them. Just as the house is about to be washed away, the magician returns home, furious, and reverses the spell.*

Puccini, Giacomo
(1858–1924)

Puccini was an Italian opera composer. He had a gift for writing emotional operas that audiences love. They are full of rich orchestral music and soaring melodies for the singers. His four greatest works, *La Bohème*, *Tosca*, *Madame Butterfly* and *Turandot*, are among the most popular operas ever written.

 Listen to the gentle 'Humming Chorus' from *Madame Butterfly*.

Puccini's colourful opera Madame Butterfly *is set in Japan. Like many of his operas, it tells the story of a tragic love affair.*

pulse
See **beat**.

punk rock
Punk rock was aggressive rock music with angry lyrics and a violent heavy beat. In the 1970s, punk groups like The Sex Pistols, The Clash and The Damned wanted to shock people. They wore safety pins through their skin, had wildly coloured Mohican haircuts, and behaved as badly as they could.

Purcell, Henry
(1659–1695)

Purcell was the greatest English composer before **Elgar**. As a boy he sang in the choir of the Royal Chapel, and became organist of Westminster Abbey aged 20. In his short life he wrote all sorts of pieces, including church music, pieces to celebrate royal occasions and lively dances for the theatre. His opera *Dido and Aeneas* was the first important English opera.

'Dido's Lament' from *Dido and Aeneas* and the 'Frost music' from *King Arthur* both show how imaginative Purcell was at matching music to words.

quartet
A quartet is a group of four performers, or a piece for four performers. The **string quartet** is one of the most important forms of **chamber music**. Many small jazz groups are quartets, usually consisting of piano, double bass, drums and sax (saxophone).

quintet
A quintet is a group of five musicians who sing or play together, or a piece for five players. You will often hear wind quintets (flute, oboe, clarinet, horn and bassoon) and string quintets (**string quartet** plus an extra viola or cello) at chamber music concerts.

The most popular quintet of all is Schubert's sunny 'Trout' Quintet. Its fourth movement is a set of **variations** on his song of the same name.

A 1990s punk rock group at a gig in New York.

Rachmaninov, Sergey

(1873–1943)

Rachmaninov was a Russian composer, and one of the finest concert pianists of all time. He almost gave up composing after the first performance of his First Symphony was a failure because the conductor was drunk. Rachmaninov regained his confidence after hypnosis and wrote his Second Piano Concerto, two more symphonies and two more piano concertos.

Rachmaninov's Second Piano Concerto is the best-loved piano concerto of all. It is full of rich tunes that rise and fall with melting sadness.

raga

A raga is a type of **scale** used in Indian music. The word *raga* means 'to please', and each raga creates a particular mood or mental picture. Different ragas are played at different times of the day.
See also **improvisation**.

These are the notes of a raga called 'bilaval' which is meant to be played in the afternoon. The mood of the players' improvisation based on this raga should be pleasant and joyful.

ragtime

Ragtime is a light-hearted style of piano music. The tune is played by the right hand, and set against a strict, steady **beat** in the left hand. (This is called **syncopation**.)

The best-known rags are by Scott Joplin (1868–1917). The most famous is 'The Entertainer', which became very popular again in 1973 as the theme tune for a film called *The Sting*.

Ragtime was first popular in American bars around the year 1900, and later led to jazz.

Ravel wrote a fairy-tale opera about the magic world of childhood, called L'Enfant et les Sortilèges *(The Child and the Magic Spells). It includes talking teapots, dancing bats, an arithmetical chorus, a singing squirrel and a singing frog.*

rap

Rap developed in the 1970s, when New York DJs started to recite words rhythmically over a strong backing beat. The rapper often makes up the words on the spot. Raps are often funny and light-hearted, though 'gangsta' rap is angry and aggressive.

In the 1980s, rap was part of the trendy New York hip hop scene along with break-dancing, training shoes, skateboards and pop graffiti.

rave music

A rave is a huge dance party that often lasts all night. Raves are held in large buildings like empty warehouses or disused aircraft hangars. Non-stop electronic music pounds out a very fast beat in time with flashing lights.
See **techno**.

Ravel, Maurice

(1875–1937)

Ravel was a French composer who was fascinated by the clever workings of mechanical toys. His own pieces are carefully put together in just the same way. Ravel loved Spain, and some of his music has an exotic Spanish flavour.

When a pianist friend lost his right arm in the First World War, Ravel helped his career by composing a piano concerto for left hand only.

Ravel's *Boléro* is a Spanish dance with an insistent rhythmic **ostinato**. For something more gentle, try the delicate *Pavane pour une infante défunte*. It is a slow dance for a dead Spanish princess.

recitative

Recitative is singing that follows speech rhythms. The singer recites the words quite fast, often singing mainly on one note. In **opera** and **oratorio** composers use recitative to tell the story or to hold conversations quickly, so the action is not delayed. Recitatives are usually followed by **arias**.

recorder

The recorder is a hollow tube of wood or plastic. It has several holes and a block at one end to make a narrow opening. As you blow down this end, the blown air vibrates and produces **sound** waves. Different notes are produced by covering and opening the holes.

There are four recorders in a recorder quartet. The descant is the highest-pitched, and the one most people learn to play first. The treble is lower-pitched, and is most often used for solo playing. Next comes the tenor, and then the bass.

More children play the descant recorder than any other instrument. Every year, over 60 million are made and sold all over the world.

recording

In 1877 Thomas Edison invented the gramophone. Before that the only way to hear music was to play it yourself or listen to a live performance. Edison found a way of converting the vibrations of sound into grooves on a revolving cylinder, and then playing the sounds back from it.

Modern sound recording does the same kind of thing, but reproduces the sounds so well that you can shut your eyes as you listen to your favourite band on CD and imagine they are in the same room as you!

When they are being recorded, the performers' instruments and voices are picked up by microphones which turn the sound vibrations into electronic signals. Each performer can be recorded separately on a different 'track'.

△ *A recording session in progress. The performers are in a separate studio behind a soundproof glass screen.*

The sound engineer balances sound from the tracks and mixes them together. The sound signals are stored on Digital Audio Tape (DAT) or computer disk. These record the measurements of sound waves in the form of numbers ('digits').

The producer organizes the musicians and engineers, and decides with the performers which are the best versions (called 'takes') of the music they have recorded.

After the recording session a final DAT master tape is produced. CDs and cassettes are reproduced from the master tape, ready to be sold in shops.
See also **CD**, **pop**, **sound**.

reed

A reed is a thin piece of cane, metal or plastic. Woodwind instruments like the oboe, clarinet and bassoon have reeds in their mouthpieces. The reed vibrates when air is blown over it, producing sound.
See also **instruments** (woodwind family), **sound**.

reggae

Reggae music developed in the slums of Jamaica in the late 1960s. It started as black protest music, often criticizing poverty and poor social conditions. The reggae style developed from a mixture of **soul**, **calypso**, **rhythm 'n' blues** and **rock 'n' roll**. It is warm and relaxed, with words in Jamaican dialect sung over a steady, repetitive beat.

◁ *The Jamaican reggae singer Bob Marley. In the 1970s he and his group The Wailers made reggae internationally famous.*

rehearsal

A rehearsal is when people come together to practise their performance. The very last rehearsal for musicals and operas is called the 'dress rehearsal', because the singers dress in their costumes.

religious music

For thousands of years music has been associated with religious ceremonies and magic. All over the world a single bell or drumbeat is used to call people to worship. Other music helps to create a mood for meditation and prayer, or for occasions like weddings and funerals. In India and the Far East, music accompanies temple dancing. In Africa, tribal music can be an important way of pleasing spirits or of driving away demons.

Religious music usually involves singing. Singing simple chants and **hymns** enables people to feel part of religious ceremonies. In Jewish synagogues a precentor leads the singing, using his voice in a very dramatic and emotional way. Christian churches have **choirs**, and modern Christian worship sometimes includes hymns in jazz and pop styles. In mosques a *muzzein* chants the call to prayer from the top of a minaret.

Many composers have written music for Christian church services, from **Gregorian chant** to large choral works using the words of the **mass** or **requiem**.
See also **carol**, **gospel music**, **spiritual**.

Allegri's *Miserere*, Fanshawe's *African Sanctus*, Verdi's 'Dies irae' from his *Requiem*, and Gregorian chant.

◁ *Buddhist monks play a pair of Tibetan trumpets.*

requiem

The requiem is the Roman Catholic church service in memory of the dead. It is often set to music. The words are in Latin and include dramatic passages describing death, the Day of Judgement and heaven.

 Listen to extracts from the three most famous requiems, by Mozart, Fauré and Verdi.

rest

See **notation**.

rhythms

Rhythms are patterns of sounds and silences. In western music, rhythms usually fit against a steady beat or pulse. Our bodies often want to move in time to strong rhythms, which is why rhythm is so important in **dance music** and pop.
See also **syncopation**.

rhythm 'n' blues

Rhythm 'n' blues is a type of **jazz** that developed in the 1950s. 'R & B' (as it is called) combined elements of rural **blues** with urban jazz. It was amplified, and accompanied by electric guitars. Rhythm 'n' blues developed into **rock 'n' roll**.

rock

Nowadays the term 'rock' means pop music that is more serious than chart music. It is often based on expert guitar playing and aimed at older listeners. Rock developed from **rock 'n' roll**, which was the basic style of early pop music.

rock 'n' roll

Rock 'n' roll was created in the mid-1950s when white musicians started playing **rhythm 'n' blues**. Singers like Elvis **Presley** mixed R & B with **country** music, giving it a faster driving beat and a new sex appeal. Rock 'n' roll singers were usually accompanied by two electric guitars, a bass guitar and drums. When rock 'n' roll took off, stars like Bill Haley and the Comets, Elvis and Buddy Holly were idolized by huge fan clubs. A Chuck Berry song was carried aboard the Voyager space probe in 1977 as an example of Earth music.

 Try 'Rock around the Clock' (Bill Haley and the Comets), 'Heartbreak Hotel' (Elvis Presley), and 'Peggy Sue' (Buddy Holly).

▽ *In the 1960s teenagers were mad about rock 'n' roll, all the more because their parents usually objected to it.*

Rodgers and Hammerstein

Many famous American **musicals** were written by the partnership of composer Richard Rodgers (1902–1979) and lyricist Oscar Hammerstein (1895–1960).

Rodgers and Hammerstein's musical The Sound of Music *contains their two best-known songs, 'The Hills Are Alive' and 'Do-Re-Mi'. It tells the real-life story of a family of Austrian children and their escape from the Nazis in the Second World War.*

In the 1940s and 50s Rodgers and Hammerstein produced a string of hit shows. Try *Oklahoma!*, *South Pacific* and *The Sound of Music*.

rondo

A rondo is an instrumental piece in which the main tune comes back several times. In between, there are contrasting sections of other music.

Rossini, Gioachino

(1792–1868)

Rossini was an Italian composer whose operas delighted audiences all over Europe. He had a sparkling sense of fun that bubbles over in his comic works. His genius for writing tunes meant he could compose whole operas in a fortnight. But at the age of 37 he gave up composing, perhaps because of exhaustion. For the remaining 40 years of his life he wrote only a few more pieces.

Rossini's **overture** *William Tell* is an irresistible example of his brilliant music.

Rolling Stones, The

The Rolling Stones are a British rock group from the 1960s. They were formed by Mick Jagger, their lead singer, and teenagers immediately loved their noisy, rebellious style. They are still hugely popular.

'Brown Sugar', 'Satisfaction', 'Jumpin' Jack Flash'

round

A round is a piece in which all parts sing the same tune. The voices enter in turn, overlapping with each other. Each voice starts the tune again as soon as it finishes, going round and round.

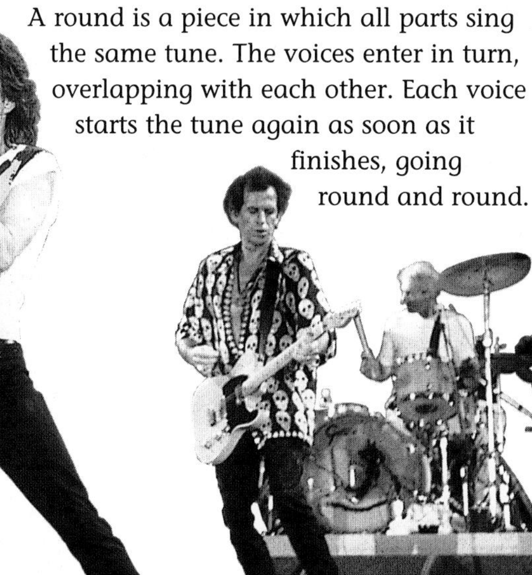

The Rolling Stones, with Mick Jagger, their swaggering lead singer.

Romantic music

European music written between 1830 and 1900 is called Romantic music. Despite its name, it is not just about love but is full of all sorts of powerful feelings. The most famous Romantic composers were Liszt, Berlioz, Schumann, Tchaikovsky and Wagner. They wrote dramatic music that often tells stories about tragedy, nature, passion or magic.
See also **programme music**.

Saint-Saëns, Camille

(1835–1921)
Saint-Saëns was a French composer who was also a brilliant pianist and organist. He is best known for his delightful collection of pieces called *Le Carnaval des Animaux* (Carnival of the Animals). He wrote them as a joke for some friends.

sampler

A sampler is a machine which records short extracts of sounds, voices or music. These sounds are processed electronically so that they can be altered and controlled through a keyboard.
See also **electronic music and instruments, house music, recording**.

scale

A scale is a series of notes arranged from lowest to highest, and back again. There are many different scales throughout the world.
See also **raga**.

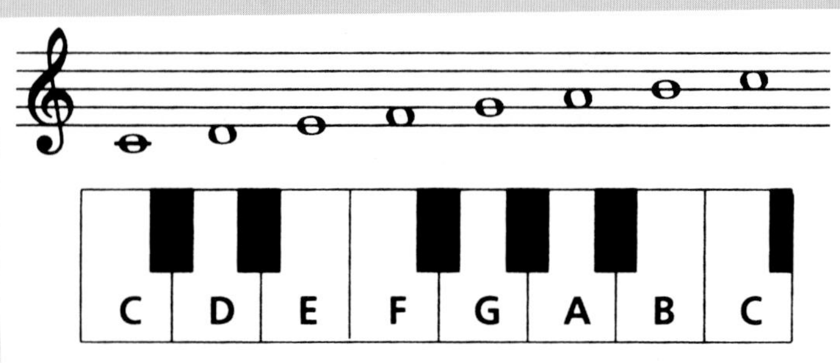

The scale most often used in Western music is the one you will hear if you play the white notes of a keyboard from one C up to the next C.

A 'chromatic scale' has twelve notes, each a semitone apart from the next.

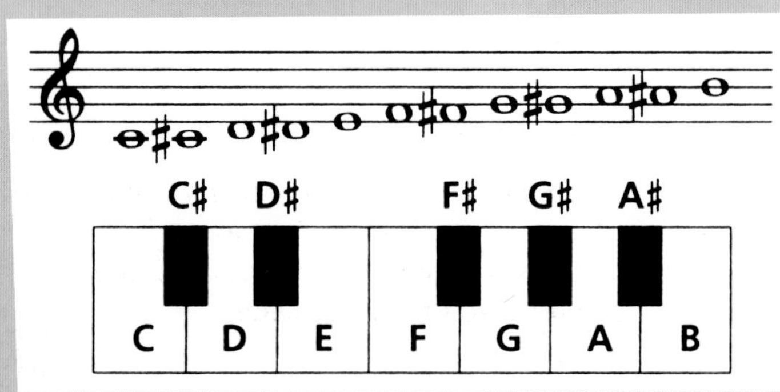

scat

Scat is a type of wordless singing used in **jazz**. The singer imitates instruments, singing nonsense phrases like 'dooby dooby do' or 'doo-wap doo-wa'. Scat singing can be very fast, sounding like a musical tongue-twister.

Scat was invented by accident. One day Louis **Armstrong** put down his trumpet to sing but forgot the words, so he made up some nonsense sounds instead.

scherzo

A scherzo is a fast, light-hearted piece of music. It is often the third movement in a **sonata** or symphony. 'Scherzo' is the Italian word for a joke.

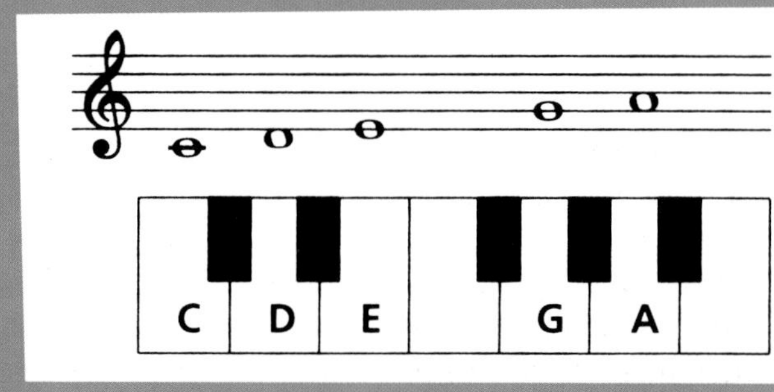

A 'pentatonic scale' is made up of five notes. The notes C, D, E, G, A form a pentatonic scale that is very common in Chinese and Scottish music.

Schoenberg, Arnold

(1874–1951)

Schoenberg was an Austrian composer. He invented a revolutionary sort of modern music called **twelve-note music**. There were riots at concerts because people disliked his music so much. Now, though, he is recognized as one of the great figures of modern music.

Schubert, Franz

(1797–1828)

The Austrian composer Franz Schubert had a natural talent for writing lovely tunes. He poured out a huge amount of music in his short life. Much of it was written for his friends to perform at home or in the coffee-houses of Vienna. Schubert wrote about 600 *Lieder* (the German word for songs). Many of them cleverly use the piano accompaniment to illustrate the words.

Try Schubert's unfinished Eighth Symphony. No one knows why he abandoned it after the first two movements.

Schumann, Robert and Clara

Robert (1810–1856) and Clara (1819–1896)

Schumann were husband and wife. Robert was one of the great composers of Romantic music, writing beautiful songs and piano pieces. Clara became one of the most famous 19th-century pianists. She was the daughter of Robert's piano teacher, who tried to stop them marrying. Robert suffered from mental illness, and eventually died in a mental home two years after trying to drown himself.

Robert Schumann's *Kinderscenen* are short, dreamy piano pieces based on scenes from childhood.

score

The score of a piece is the written or printed copy showing the music of all the performers together. The score is used by the **conductor**, who needs to see what everyone should be playing. Each performer has a separate piece of music that just shows their own part. See also **graphic score**.

The first page of the score of Mahler's Sixth Symphony, in his own handwriting.

semitone

On a keyboard, a semitone is the smallest step from any black or white key to the next one above or below it.

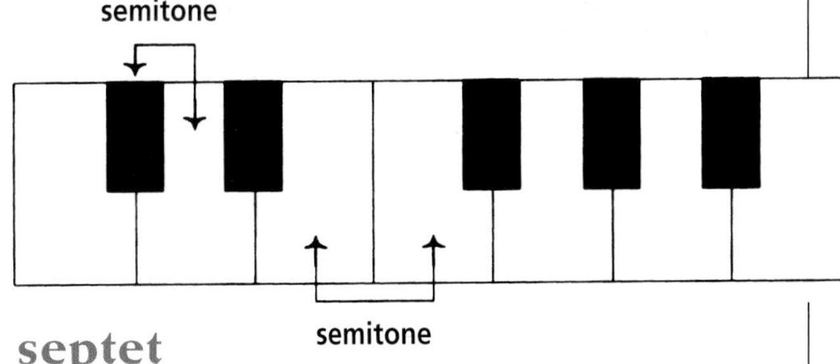

septet

A septet is a group of seven players or a piece for seven instruments.

serenade

A serenade is a lovesong to be sung under a lady's window at night-time, often accompanied by guitar. A serenade is also a set of short, light-hearted pieces for instruments.

sextet

Groups of six players and pieces for six instruments are called sextets.

 Try the cheeky Sextet for wind quintet and piano by the French composer Poulenc.

shanty

A shanty is a sailors' song. The strong rhythms of sea shanties helped sailors keep together when pulling the ship's ropes. The best-known sea shanty is 'What Shall we do with the Drunken Sailor?'

Shostakovich, Dmitri

(1906–1975)

When the Russian composer Shostakovich was a student, he was so poor that he had to earn money playing the piano in cinemas for silent films. Then his First Symphony made him famous at the age of just 20. After that he was the former Soviet Union's leading composer. However, he was often criticized for not writing the sort of music that communist politicians like Stalin wanted. He lost faith in them, and his later music is often dark and bitter.

Like much of his music, Shostakovich's Piano Concerto No. 2 is sometimes light-hearted and sarcastic, sometimes sad.

singing

Singing is the most natural way of making music. People sing in different ways. Opera singers train their voices to be powerful and fill big halls. Pop and jazz singers use microphones and sing more naturally. Arabic, Chinese and Indian singers all have their own special ways of singing. See also **choir**, **opera**, **scat**, **song**, **voice**.

soloist

A soloist is someone who plays or sings on their own. Sometimes a soloist will be accompanied by an orchestra, as in a **concerto**.

sonata

A sonata is an instrumental piece for a **soloist** or a few players. It usually has several **movements** of different types and speeds, often fast–slow–fast.

 Listen to Mozart's Piano Sonata in C major or Beethoven's *Spring* Sonata for violin and piano.

song

A song is a short piece of music for voice. It usually has a number of different verses. There are many different types of songs. Folk songs are very old songs that were taught from memory long before being written down. Work songs were sung in time to the hard labour of workmen or sailors (see **shanty**). Ballads were once songs that told stories, and nowadays are slow love songs. Pop songs are often ballads, as well as covering a range of other topics. See also **aria**, **hymn**, **lullaby**, **spiritual**, **voice**.

The opera singer Jessye Norman, pouring out her feelings as she sings.

song cycle

A song cycle is a group of songs which are performed together. They often tell a continuous story, or are about the same subject.

soprano

Soprano is the name of the highest female voice, or the highest member of a family of instruments. Soprano is pitched above **alto**. A boy's soprano voice is called **treble**.

soul

Soul music mixes the styles of black American **gospel** and **blues** singing with rock 'n' roll accompaniments. The singing is intense and emotional, and soul was a strong influence on the hi-energy disco sounds of the 1970s.

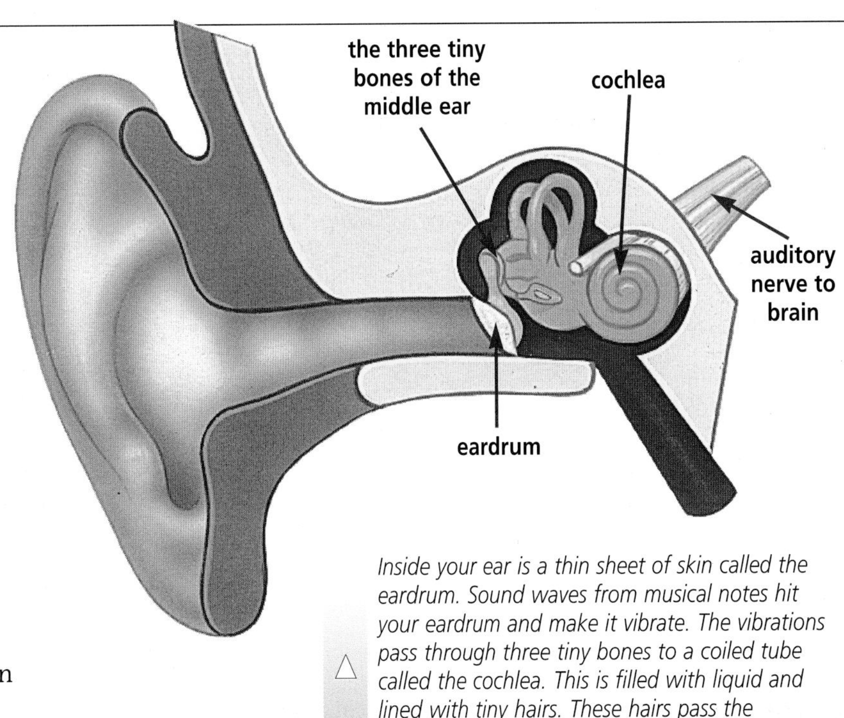

Inside your ear is a thin sheet of skin called the eardrum. Sound waves from musical notes hit your eardrum and make it vibrate. The vibrations pass through three tiny bones to a coiled tube called the cochlea. This is filled with liquid and lined with tiny hairs. These hairs pass the vibrations to the auditory nerve, which sends a description of the sound waves to your brain.

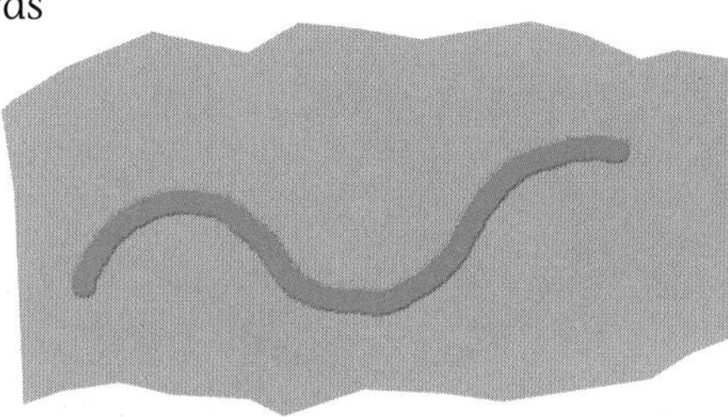

flute sound wave

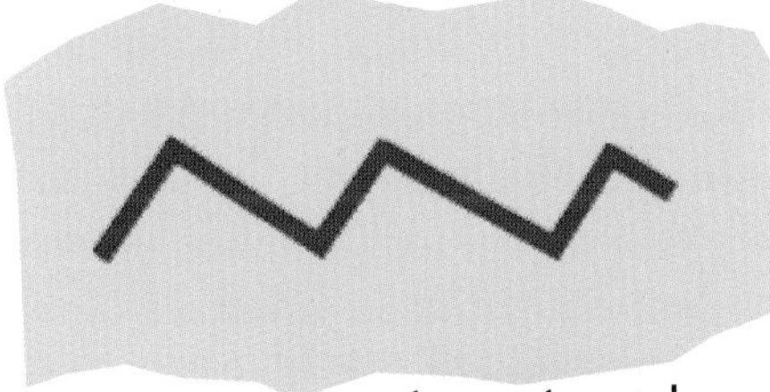

trumpet sound wave

clarinet sound wave

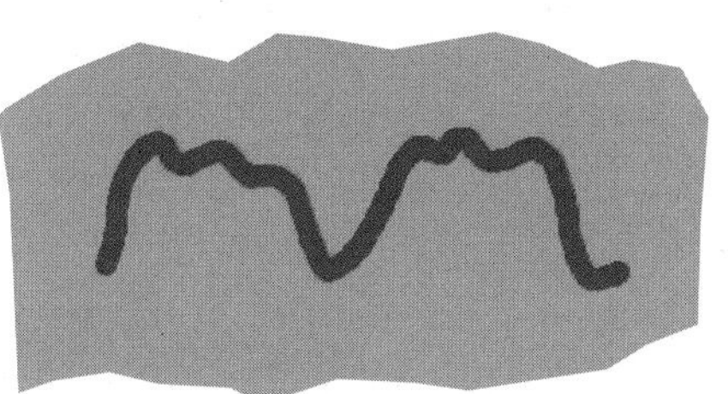

violin sound wave

Musical instruments vibrate in different ways, producing sound waves of different shapes. The type of sound wave tells the ear about the quality (or timbre) of an instrument's sound (harsh or mellow, reedy or fluty, and so on).

sound

Sounds are vibrations in the air. When musical instruments are hit, plucked, scraped or blown, they vibrate. They make the air around them vibrate too, producing variations in air pressure called 'sound waves'.

The faster the air's vibrations, the higher the sound. Longer strings and pipes produce slower vibrations and deeper sounds. The lowest musical sounds are made by organ pipes that are 32 feet long.

See also **instruments**.

spiritual

Spirituals are American religious songs. Africans who had been sold into slavery in America found comfort and hope in singing spirituals, which promised them happiness in heaven.

Famous spirituals include 'Swing Low, Sweet Chariot', and 'Go, Tell it on the Mountain'.

steel band

A steel band is a group of metal drums (called 'pans') made from old oil drums. The oil drums are cut to different lengths, and each one is tuned to produce a number of different notes.
See also **calypso**.

△ *Steel bands originally came from the Caribbean islands of Trinidad and Tobago. This one includes a pair of bongos and a drum kit.*

Strauss, Johann

(1825–1899)

Johann Strauss's father (also called Johann) was an Austrian composer. But he tried to stop his son following in his footsteps. Young Johann took a job in a bank, secretly learning the violin and studying composing. He went on to write some of the best-loved **waltz** tunes, and because of their popularity he was known as 'The Waltz King'.

 Johann Strauss's most famous composition is the *Blue Danube* waltz.

Strauss, Richard

(1864–1949)

Richard Strauss (who was no relation to Johann) was a German composer. Early in his career he wrote a series of brilliant 'symphonic poems'. They are orchestral pieces that use colourful music to tell stories. Strauss also wrote 15 operas, the most famous being the gorgeous *Der Rosenkavalier* ('The Knight of the Rose').

Listen to the waltzes from *Der Rosenkavalier* or the stunning opening of the symphonic poem *Also Sprach Zarathustra* (used in the film *2001: A Space Odyssey*).

Stravinsky, Igor

(1882–1971)

The Russian composer Stravinsky is one of the most important figures of 20th-century music. He became world-famous with three ballets, *The Firebird*, *Petrushka* and *The Rite of Spring*. The savage music of the last of these changed the course of musical history and caused a riot at its first performance.

Listen to the magical ballet *The Firebird* or the little *Greetings Prelude*, a musical joke on the tune of 'Happy Birthday'.

string instruments

See **instruments** (string family).

string quartet

A string quartet is a group of two violinists, a viola player and a cellist. Pieces composed for this group are also called string quartets.

suite

A suite is a collection of short instrumental pieces. They can usually be played either as a set or individually.

Try Bach's Orchestral Suite in D and Ravel's suite *Le Tombeau de Couperin*.

swing

Swing is a type of jazz. It was first played by **big bands** in the 1930s, when Duke **Ellington** wrote a song called 'It Don't Mean a Thing if it Ain't got that Swing'. If someone says 'Swing it!' they're telling you to play in a relaxed and groovy way.

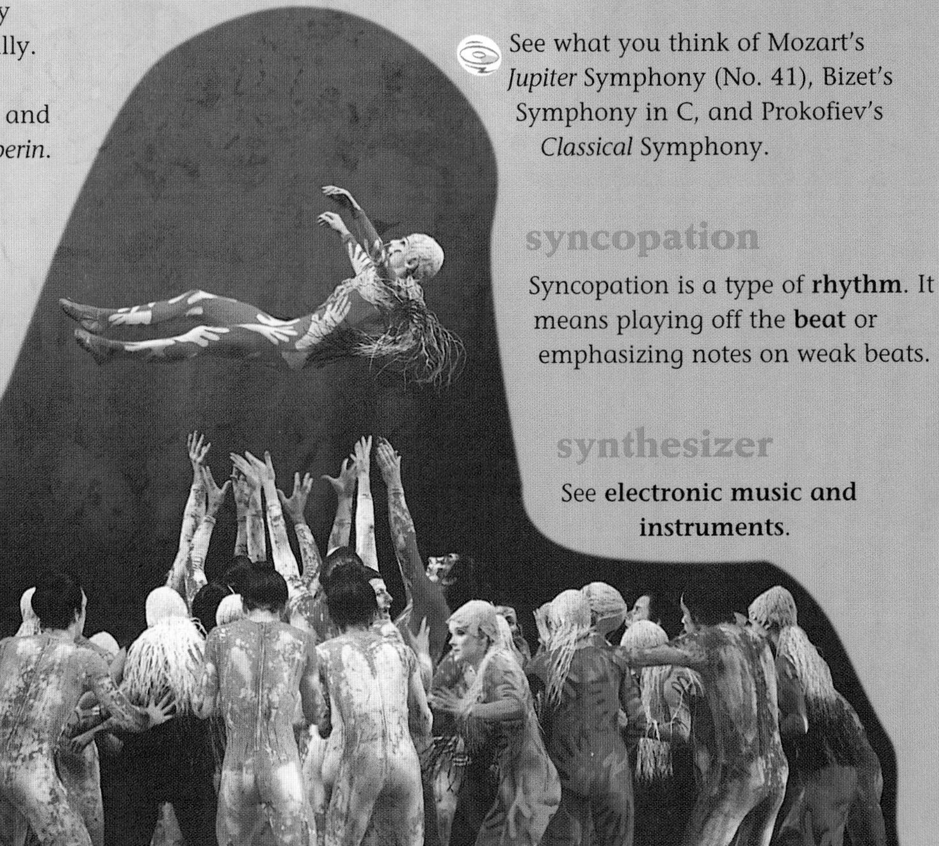

▽ *In Stravinsky's ballet The Rite of Spring, ferocious music and dance depict an ancient tribe celebrating the triumph of spring over winter.*

symphony

A symphony is a substantial piece of music for an orchestra, often lasting for half an hour or longer.

A symphony is usually divided up into four sections, called movements. The first movement is usually fast and lively, while the second is slow. The third is often light-hearted, and the last is often in **rondo** form, providing a fast and exciting ending. Of course, composers do not always stick to this pattern. For example, the last movement of Tchaikovsky's Sixth Symphony ends very slowly and quietly.

Haydn and **Mozart** were two of the greatest symphony composers. Haydn wrote 104, and Mozart 41. **Beethoven** wrote the first of his nine great symphonies in 1800. Later composers continued to make the symphony more dramatic, using bigger orchestras to create richer sounds. Other great symphony composers of the 19th century were **Schubert**, **Brahms**, **Dvorák**, Bruckner and **Tchaikovsky**.

In the 20th century, composers began to experiment more in their symphonies. **Mahler** composed gigantic symphonies that included choirs and solo singers. Other great symphonic composers are **Elgar**, **Vaughan Williams**, **Shostakovich** and **Tippett**.

See what you think of Mozart's *Jupiter* Symphony (No. 41), Bizet's Symphony in C, and Prokofiev's *Classical* Symphony.

syncopation

Syncopation is a type of **rhythm**. It means playing off the **beat** or emphasizing notes on weak beats.

synthesizer

See **electronic music and instruments**.

T

tarantella

The tarantella is an Italian dance. It is said to be named after the tarantula spider. Dancing the tarantella was supposed to make you sweat out the poison from the spider's bite.

Three famous tenors: Luciano Pavarotti, José Carreras and Plácido Domingo.

Tchaikovsky, Peter Ilyich

(1840–1893)

Tchaikovsky is many people's favourite composer. His music is full of emotion and packed with lovely tunes. For 14 years he composed with the financial support of a rich lady who loved his music, though they never met. Tchaikovsky is best known for his six symphonies and the colourful ballets *Swan Lake* and *The Nutcracker*. His unhappy love life was the source of the sadness in some of his music, particularly in his tragic Sixth Symphony.

Tchaikovsky's two most popular pieces are the fantasy-overture *Romeo and Juliet* and the *1812 Overture*.

Clara, heroine of Tchaikovsky's ballet The Nutcracker.

techno music

'Techno' is short for 'technology'. Techno music uses electronic instruments and sounds from **samplers**. At **raves** it is fast and rhythmic, for dancing. But it can also be quiet and relaxing, and sometimes linked to visual images. This is called 'ambient' music.

tempo

The tempo of a piece of music is the speed at which it is played.

tenor

Tenor is the name of a male **voice** (or an instrument) with a medium to low range. Tenor is pitched below **alto** and above **bass**.

theory

Music theory is the study of how music works. If you study theory, you learn how to compose. You also learn about **notation**, **harmony**, orchestration and **acoustics**.

timbre

Timbre (pronounced *taam-bre*) is the particular quality of a **sound**. If you play the same note on a recorder and then on a glockenspiel, you can hear that the timbre of the sounds is different, although the notes are the same.

timpani

See **instruments** (percussion family).

Tippett, Michael

(born 1905)

Sir Michael Tippett is one of the great figures of 20th-century British music. Tippett's strong personal beliefs have influenced much of his music. He refused to fight in the Second World War and his moving **oratorio** *A Child of Our Time* deals with good and evil. It includes some well-known **spirituals** for chorus.

Try 'Ritual Dances' from *The Midsummer Marriage*, or the *Fantasia Concertante on a theme of Corelli.*

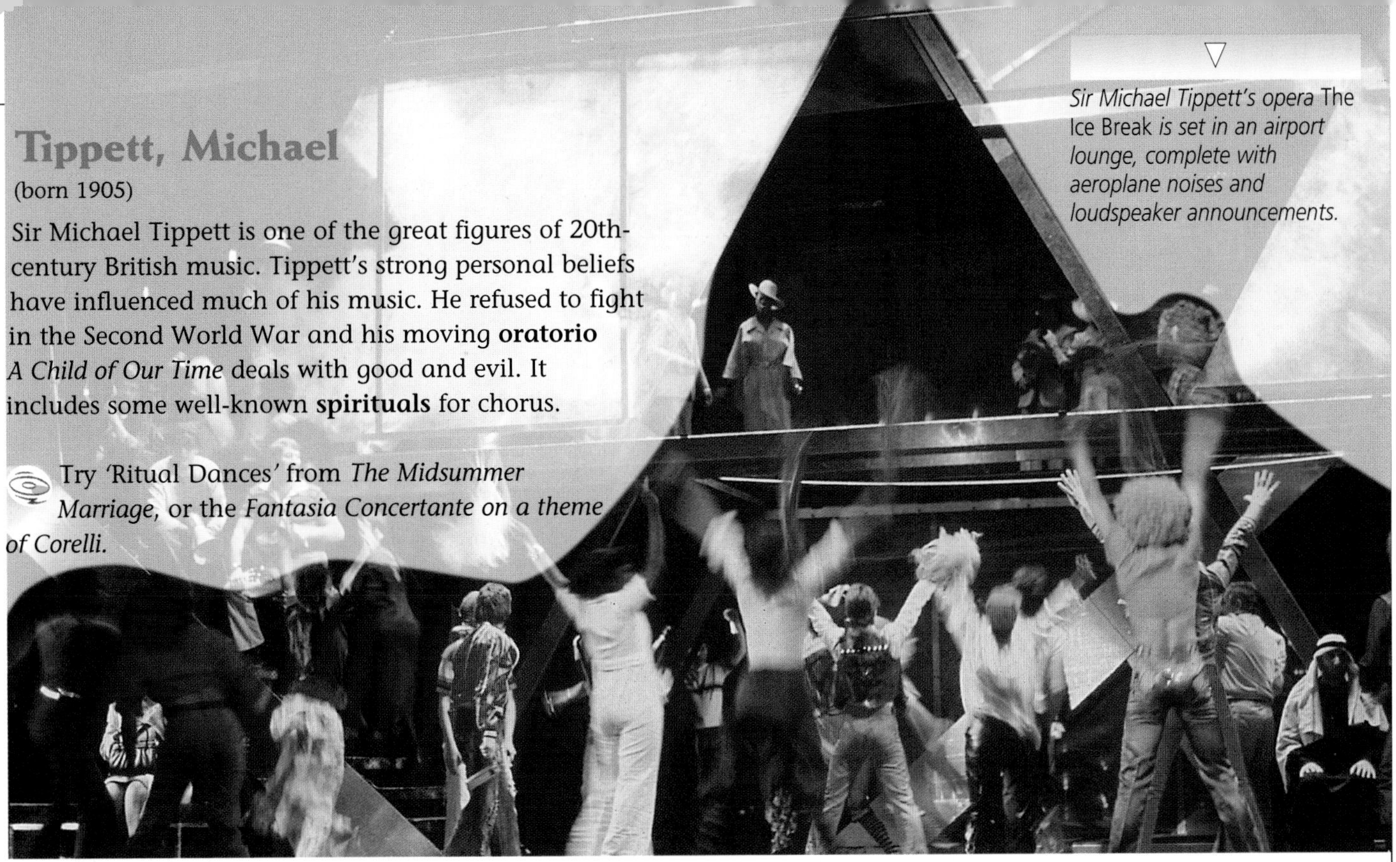

Sir Michael Tippett's opera The Ice Break *is set in an airport lounge, complete with aeroplane noises and loudspeaker announcements.*

toccata

A toccata is a keyboard piece intended to show off the player's skill. The first toccatas were improvisations, with lots of fast and difficult music.

Try the two most famous toccatas for organ, one by J.S. Bach and one by a French composer called Widor.

tone

If you look at a keyboard, a tone is any step of two **semitones**. Tone can also mean the kind of sound produced by a performer or an instrument.

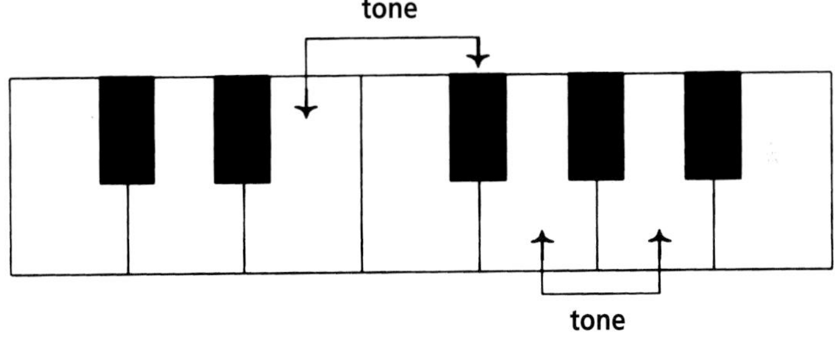

treble

A treble is a boy **soprano**. The treble recorder plays notes that are lower than the descant recorder but higher than the tenor recorder.

trill

A trill is a type of **ornament**. It sounds like a fast warble between a note and the next note above or below it.

trio

A trio is a group of three people singing or playing together. A piece for three performers is also called a trio.

Listen to Poulenc's Trio for piano, oboe and bassoon.

tuning

Tuning an instrument means adjusting it to a fixed **pitch**. Performers must take care to play or sing 'in tune' with each other.

A two-pronged piece of metal called a tuning fork produces an accurate note for performers to check that they are in tune.

twelve-note music

Twelve-note (or twelve-tone) music is music composed using a method invented by the composer Arnold **Schoenberg**. He based each piece around a different order of all twelve notes (seven white and five black) of the chromatic **scale**. Twelve-note music sounds extremely modern and jarring at first, until you get used to it.

U

unison

When people play or sing the same notes or the same tune together, this is called singing or playing in unison.

variations

Variations are versions of the same tune (or 'theme') that are altered in different ways. Variations come in sets, and each variation does something new to the theme. Sometimes you can recognize it, and sometimes it is heavily disguised.

Vaughan Williams, Ralph

(1872–1958)

Ralph Vaughan Williams was an English composer. He loved English **folk music** and travelled the country collecting folk songs. These were a strong influence on his own pieces. Because of this his music is often associated with the beauty of the English countryside.

Try the *Fantasia on Greensleeves* and *The Lark Ascending.*

Verdi, Giuseppe

(1813–1901)

Verdi was one of the greatest opera composers. His gift for stirring tunes and noble or tragic stories made him an Italian national hero. For a time he was a member of the national parliament, and 28,000 people came to his funeral. Apart from his operas, Verdi's most famous work is his dramatic *Requiem*.
See also **opera.**

vibrato

Vibrato is a slight up-and-down wavering of the **pitch** of a note. String players, wind players and singers use vibrato to make their sound richer and more expressive.

virtuoso

A virtuoso is an outstandingly brilliant performer.

The violin virtuoso Anne-Sophie Mutter.

V

Vivaldi, Antonio

(1678–1741)

Vivaldi was a leading Italian composer of **baroque music**. He lived and worked in Venice, teaching music at a girls' orphanage that had a famous choir and orchestra. Many of his pieces were written for his pupils. He wrote more than 500 concertos for all sorts of instruments, but particularly the violin.

Vivaldi's *The Four Seasons* is a group of four short violin concertos. They are an early example of **programme music**, depicting autumn, winter, spring and summer.

voice

Your voice is your very own instrument. It produces sound when air from your lungs vibrates the vocal cords in your throat. The air in the hollow spaces (cavities) of your chest, throat and mouth vibrates and amplifies (makes louder) the sound of your voice.

sound vibrates in nose and mouth cavities
vocal cords vibrate in throat to produce sound
lungs inside chest cavity pump air
diaphragm muscle expands and contracts lungs

Men's voices are deeper than women's because their vocal cords are longer. As a boy gets older, his vocal cords grow and his voice changes (or 'breaks') from high to low.

There are four basic types of voice. **Soprano** and **alto** are the higher and lower female (or boys') voices. **Tenor** and **bass** are the higher and lower men's voices.

Wagner, Richard

(1813–1883)

Wagner's operas have plots about the gods and superheroes of ancient legends. They are very long and use a huge orchestra. Wagner wanted to control all aspects of opera, from the **libretto** to the stage designs and production. His ideas led him to build his own opera house at Bayreuth in Germany.

Try the spectacular *Ride of the Valkyrie*, and *Siegfried's Funeral Music.*

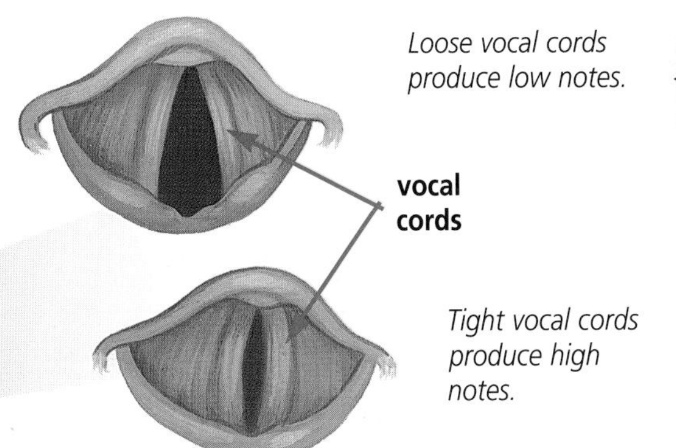

Loose vocal cords produce low notes.

Tight vocal cords produce high notes.

Walton, William

(1902–1983)

The English composer William Walton became famous overnight after performances of his *Façade Entertainment*. People were shocked because the poems in it were read through a megaphone over the music.

Walton had a gift for writing memorable **film music**, full of stirring tunes, energetic rhythms and tender moments. His best-known piece is the noble march *Crown Imperial*, written for the coronation of Queen Elizabeth II.

waltz

A waltz is a type of dance. One strong beat is followed by two lighter ones. You can always recognize waltzes from their dancing 'tum ti ti, tum ti ti' rhythm.

See also **Strauss (Johann)**.

wind band

A wind band (or wind orchestra) is a large group of brass, wind and percussion instruments. Except for a double bass, there are no string instruments.

See also **military band**.

woodwind instruments

See **instruments** (woodwind family).

Walton's thrilling oratorio Belshazzar's Feast *tells the story of the biblical city of Babylon. The night before its destruction, a ghostly hand appeared to King Belshazzar and wrote on the wall a prophecy of the city's downfall.*

World music

Everywhere in the world people can hear western **pop** and **classical** music on the radio and television. But 'world music' describes the many other kinds of music to be found in various countries. World music is often based on a country's traditional music, and it is usually performed on instruments from the region, with songs sung in the local language. Though it is often **folk** music, it can also be in a country's pop or classical style.

Africa

Modern African music is a vibrant mix of traditional African music and other styles that were brought into the country by settlers from abroad. Traditional songs and dances still play a special part in everyday African life. There are songs for all occasions: work songs, wedding songs, and lullabies. Rhythm is also a vital part of African music. Drums accompany singing and dancing, and they are also used to accompany story-telling.

Europe

Each European country has its own traditional music. Instruments such as the fiddle (violin), accordion, and **zither** are popular everywhere. Some countries have special instruments which make the music of that country very distinctive, such as the Greek bouzouki (a type of guitar), the bagpipes of Scotland, and the alphorn of Switzerland.

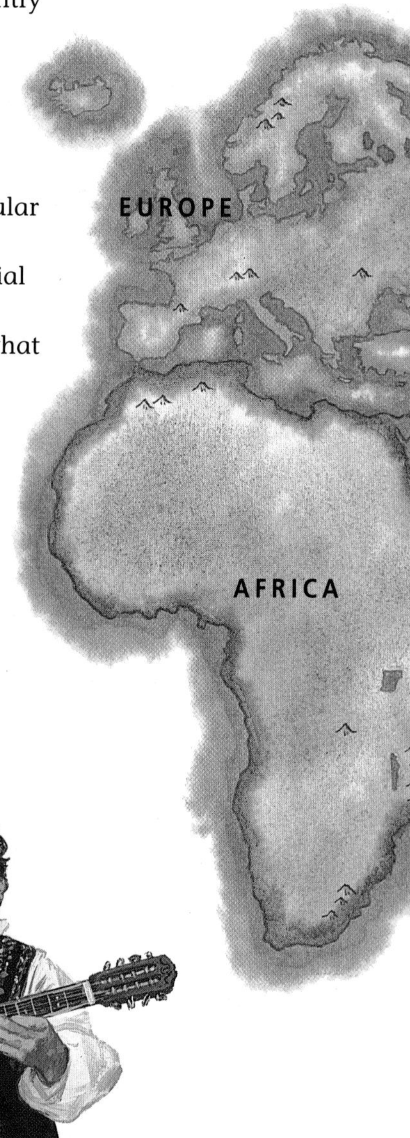

African children are taught to make and play the mbira (or thumb piano). You produce notes by flicking strips of metal with your thumbs. The metal may come from old bicycle or umbrella spokes.

The bouzouki is a Greek folk instrument with four pairs of metal strings and a long neck. It developed from a Turkish instrument called the bozuk saz.

African drums and xylophones are made from a variety of materials, and come in all shapes and sizes. The xylophone on the left is called a balafon.

EASTERN ASIA
Japan
China
INDIA
INDONESIA
AUSTRALASIA
Australia
New Zealand

Eastern Asia and Indonesia

The traditional music of Eastern Asia is usually based on pentatonic **scales**. Melody is more important than harmony, and tunes are often decorated by **improvisation**.

China and Japan both have own traditions of formal classical music, which is usually learnt by heart or improvised. Vocal music is very important in China. Stories are chanted to music, and there is a colourful tradition of Chinese opera.

Traditional Chinese instruments include stringed instruments such as the cheng (rather like a **zither**) and pipa. The kum qu are small drums.

Among the traditional Japanese instruments most often heard in concerts outside Japan are the koto, which has 13 silk or nylon strings plucked with a plectrum, and the shakuhachi, a bamboo flute.

India

Indian music is based on **ragas**, which are varied and decorated by **improvisation**. Performers of Indian classical music know over a hundred ragas by heart. The rhythm in Indian music is based on fixed rhythmic patterns called talas (tala means 'clap'). These are usually played on the tabla, a pair of drums. The sitar, flute and sarangi are important melody instruments. The **drone** sound is a very important part of Indian music. The tambura is the main drone instrument.

A pair of Indian musicians improvising on the sitar (left) and tabla.

Australasia

Long before European settlers arrived, the native peoples of Australia and New Zealand had their own style of music, which was an important part of their everyday life.

The music of the aborigines of Australia was mainly vocal, but accompanied by stamping and clapping. The most famous aboriginal instrument is the didgeridoo. It is a long decorated wooden trumpet that is made from a branch of the eucalyptus tree.

The Maoris of New Zealand are famous for their singing. Their traditional religious chants must be performed without any mistakes, because errors or alterations are thought to bring bad luck.

The didjeridu makes a variety of notes depending on how the player blows down it. Skilled players are able to breathe in a special way so that the sound is continous. This provides a drone accompaniment for dancing and singing.

World music

North America

Before the first settlers arrived from Europe in the 15th century, the native Americans (called 'Indians' by the newcomers) had their own songs and tribal dances. The settlers brought with them all sorts of folk and classical music from their different home countries. The music of the slaves who were shipped in from Africa became the basis of jazz, pop and rock music. The African influence was strongest in the Caribbean, where styles such as **calypso** and **reggae** became popular.

NORTH AMERICA

SOUTH AMERICA

The guitar is the main accompaniment for North American folk music. Easy-to-carry instruments like the guitar, banjo and harmonica were popular with the early settlers and the cowboys who travelled across America.

South American Indian musicians in their traditional costume playing the violin, a small harp and a simple metal flute.

South America

Some South American music continued the ancient traditions of the early Incas and Aztecs. But much of South America was conquered by Spanish and Portuguese invaders. The lilting rhythms of their music are reflected in popular dances like the tango and samba. Brazilian dance music plays a colourful part in local carnivals, making much use of lively percussion instruments like maracas, claves and drums.

xylophone

A xylophone is a tuned percussion instrument. It has wooden bars that are hit with beaters to produce different notes.

yodelling

Yodelling is a special kind of singing. It was used by cowherds to call to each other on the mountain slopes of the Swiss Alps. Yodelling is very forceful so that it can be heard from far away, echoing in the clear mountain air.

zither

A zither is a plucked string instrument used in Austrian and Bavarian folk music. The strings are stretched over a flat wooden soundbox and plucked with the fingers of the right hand.